OHIO COUNTY PUBLIC LIBRARY
WHEELING, W. VA. 26003

P9-DGK-940

OHIO COUNTY PUBLIC LIBRARY
WHEELING, W. VA. 26003

The Impeachment of Bill Clinton

by Nathan Aaseng

J
973.929
Aase
2000

AP 10 '01

FAMOUS

TRIALS

Lucent Books, San Diego, CA

1270142921

Titles in the Famous Trials series include:

The Boston Massacre
Brown v. Board of Education
Cherokee Nation v. Georgia
The Dred Scott Decision
Miranda v. Arizona
The Nuremberg Trials
The O.J. Simpson Trial
Roe v. Wade

The Rosenberg Espionage
  Case
The Salem Witch Trials
The Scopes Trial
The Trial of Adolf Eichmann
The Trial of Joan of Arc
The Trial of John Brown
The Trial of Socrates

No part of this book may be reproduced or used in any form or by any means, electrical, mechanical, or otherwise, including, but not limited to, photocopy, recording, or any information storage and retrieval system, without prior written permission from the publisher.

Library of Congress Cataloging-in-Publication Data

Aaseng, Nathan.
  The impeachment of Bill Clinton / by Nathan Aaseng.
  p. cm. — (Famous trials)
  Includes bibliographical references and index.
  Summary: Examines the impeachment of Bill Clinton, discussing the history of impeachment, his actions, the struggle in the House, the Senate trial, and the conclusion of the proceedings.
  ISBN 1-56006-651-2 (lib. bdg. : alk. paper)
  1. Clinton, Bill, 1946–   —Impeachment Juvenile literature.
  2. Trials (Impeachment)—United States Juvenile literature.
  3. United States—Politics and government—1993–
Juvenile literature. [1. Clinton, Bill, 1946–   —Impeachment.
  2. Trials (Impeachment) 3. Impeachments. 4. United States—
Politics and government—1993–] I. Title. II. Series.
E886.2.A33 2000
973.929'092—dc21   99-39568
                                                                          CIP

Copyright © 2000 by Lucent Books, Inc.
P.O. Box 289011
San Diego, CA 92198-9011
Printed in the U.S.A.

Table of Contents

Foreword

"The law is not an end in and of itself, nor does it provide ends. It is preeminently a means to serve what we think is right."

William J. Brennan Jr.

THE CONCEPT OF JUSTICE AND THE RULE OF LAW are hallmarks of Western civilization, manifested perhaps most visibly in widely famous and dramatic court trials. These trials include such important and memorable personages as the ancient Greek philosopher Socrates, who was accused and convicted of corrupting the minds of his society's youth in 399 B.C.; the French maiden and military leader Joan of Arc, accused and convicted of heresy against the church in 1431; to former football star O.J. Simpson, acquitted of double murder in 1995. These and other well-known and controversial trials constitute the most public, and therefore most familiar, demonstrations of a Western legal tradition that dates back through the ages. Although no one is certain when the first law code appeared or when the first formal court trials were held, Babylonian ruler Hammurabi introduced the first known law code in about 1760 B.C. It remains unclear how this code was administered, and no records of specific trials have survived. What is clear, however, is that humans have always sought to govern behavior and define actions in terms of law.

Almost all societies have made laws and prosecuted people for going against those laws, but the question of which behaviors to sanction and which to censure has always been controversial and remains in flux. Some, such as Roman orator and legislator Cicero, argue that laws are simply applications of universal standards. Cicero believed that humanity would agree on what constituted illegal behavior and that human laws were a mere extension of natural laws. "True law is right reason in agreement with nature," he wrote,

4

world-wide in scope, unchanging, everlasting. . . . We may not oppose or alter that law, we cannot abolish it, we cannot be freed from its obligations by any legislature. . . . This [natural] law does not differ for Rome and for Athens, for the present and for the future. . . . It is and will be valid for all nations and all times.

Cicero's rather optimistic view has been contradicted throughout history, however. For every law made to preserve harmony and set universal standards of behavior, another has been born of fear, prejudice, greed, desire for power, and a host of other motives. History is replete with individuals defying and fighting to change such laws—and even to topple governments that dictate such laws. Abolitionists fought against slavery, civil rights leaders fought for equal rights, millions throughout the world have fought for independence—these constitute a minimum of reasons for which people have sought to overturn laws that they believed to be wrong or unjust. In opposition to Cicero, then, many others, such as eighteenth-century English poet and philosopher William Godwin, believe humans must be constantly vigilant against bad laws. As Godwin said in 1793:

Laws we sometimes call the wisdom of our ancestors. But this is a strange imposition. It was as frequently the dictate of their passion, of timidity, jealousy, a monopolizing spirit, and a lust of power that knew no bounds. Are we not obliged perpetually to renew and remodel this misnamed wisdom of our ancestors? To correct it by a detection of their ignorance, and a censure of their intolerance?

Lucent Books' *Famous Trials* series showcases trials that exemplify both society's praiseworthy condemnation of universally unacceptable behavior, and its misguided persecution of individuals based on fear and ignorance, as well as trials that leave open the question of whether justice has been done. Each volume begins by setting the scene and providing a historical context to show how society's mores influence the trial process and the verdict.

Each book goes on to present a detailed and lively account of the trial, including liberal use of primary source material such as direct testimony, lawyers' summations, and contemporary and modern commentary. In addition, sidebars throughout the text create a broader context by presenting illuminating details about important points of law, information on key personalities, and important distinctions related to civil, federal, and criminal procedures. Thus, all of the primary and secondary source material included in both the text and the sidebars demonstrates to readers the sources and methods historians use to derive information and conclusions about such events.

Lastly, each *Famous Trials* volume includes one or more of the following comprehensive tools that motivate readers to pursue further reading and research. A timeline allows readers to see the scope of the trial at a glance, annotated bibliographies provide both sources for further research and a thorough list of works consulted, a glossary helps students with unfamiliar words and concepts, and a comprehensive index permits quick scanning of the book as a whole.

The insight of Oliver Wendell Holmes Jr., distinguished Supreme Court justice, exemplifies the theme of the *Famous Trials* series. Taken from *The Common Law*, published in 1881, Holmes remarked: "The life of the law has not been logic, it has been experience." That "experience" consists mainly in how laws are applied in society and challenged in the courts, a process resulting in differing outcomes from one generation to the next. Thus, the *Famous Trials* series encourages readers to examine trials within a broader historical and social context.

Introduction

An Agonizing Decision

SHOULD BILL CLINTON be impeached? No one doubted that the president had done wrong. But was his attempt to hide an affair with a White House intern a forgivable mistake in a private matter or a serious crime that made him unfit to continue in office?

As the vote on the charges against the president drew near, the issues weighed ever more heavily on the mind of Sherwood Boehlert. All around him, the battle lines were being drawn as members of the U.S. House of Representatives declared their intentions, either to impeach or to oppose the impeachment. It became obvious that the voting was going to be close. Boehlert, a sixty-two-year-old representative from upstate New York, was one of a handful of undecided lawmakers who held the president's fate in their hands.

Representative Sherwood Boehlert (New York).

Never during his eight terms in Congress had Boehlert faced such an agonizing decision. Sixteen years earlier, he had grimly cast a vote to send U.S. troops to Lebanon, knowing that his own son would be one of those soldiers put in harm's way. "But that was nothing compared to what I now face," Boehlert admitted. "With Lebanon, the right thing was clear. Here, I stay up at night and toss and turn." [1]

Only once in the history of the nation had the House of Representatives voted to impeach, or bring formal charges against, a president. That had occurred 130 years ago, and the episode had not displayed Congress in glory. Most historians viewed the impeachment and trial of Andrew Johnson in 1868 as a power play fed by personal and political hatred of the man and his policies rather than as a noble act of governing. Would history look at the current attempt to impeach in a similar light?

Boehlert had to consider the possibility that it would. The poisoned atmosphere of national politics in 1998 reminded many observers of the bitter Johnson-Congress feuds. Both Clinton supporters and Clinton opponents criticized the other side savagely. Georgia Republican Bob Barr had been calling Clinton a scoundrel long before the current scandal erupted. When he quoted former president John F. Kennedy in a speech attacking President Clinton during the impeachment debate, Kennedy's

Magazine publisher Larry Flynt offered $1 million to anyone who could provide information about the sexual misdeeds of any Republican who was attacking the president on moral grounds.

nephew Patrick was furious. The Democrat from Rhode Island confronted Barr in the hall, and a heated argument followed.

Meanwhile, magazine publisher Larry Flynt offered $1 million to anyone who could dig up some juicy sex tales about the Republicans who were attacking Clinton. As the furor raged around him, Boehlert commented bleakly, "Some people view government as war, and anything goes." [2]

Boehlert was quick to explain that no one was putting the squeeze on him to vote one way or the other. "It's not pressure from the White House promising me something. It's not pressure from leadership, threatening. It's pressure from within." [3] With calls from voters in his district split almost evenly, Boehlert had nowhere to search for answers but his soul.

On December 19, 1998, Boehlert arrived at the House of Representatives prepared to do his duty as he saw fit. He and a dozen or so moderate Republicans would decide whether to take the first step in removing the leader whom the American public had voted into the highest office in the land.

Chapter 1

History of Impeachment

THE PROBLEM OF how to deal with government officials who might be unfit for their office was only one of many technical details in the enormous task of setting up a new system of government. The authors of the Constitution debated long and hard about how to remove a government official who proved to be corrupt or dangerous.

The committee assigned to explore the issue first proposed that the president be given a seven-year term. Since this was a long time for a nation to have to deal with a leader who may be perceived as sinister after taking office, the committee suggested that an impeachment process be devised for removing such an official. Roger Sherman of Connecticut went so far as to suggest that Congress be given the power to elect the president and to remove him whenever it chose to do so.

George Mason of Virginia warned that allowing Congress to elect and fire a president would give Congress too much power. It would make the president, he said, "a mere creature of the legislature."[4] Bunning Bedford of Delaware argued for a shorter term of office so that officials who violated the public trust could be dealt with on a more regular basis by the voters.

Was the Power of Impeachment Necessary?

Eventually, the proposed Constitution shortened the term of office of the president to four years. But debate continued over whether a process of impeachment was necessary. James Iredell

After much deliberation, the Constitution committee decided to approve a provision to the Constitution that allowed for the impeachment of the president.

of North Carolina argued that it was, and that a president who committed any misdemeanor should be impeached. (Misdemeanors are the least serious offenses in the legal codes.)

The Constitution committee agreed and eventually offered a provision that the president "be removable on impeachment and conviction of mal-practice or neglect of duty." [5]

Gouverneur Morris of Pennsylvania and Charles Pinckney of South Carolina, however, sought to eliminate impeachment altogether. Pinckney believed that regular and frequent elections were the best way to get rid of a president who was not performing his duties. A president, said Pinckney, "ought not to be impeached while in office." [6]

James Madison of Virginia disagreed. He warned that even a limited term of office "was not a sufficient security," [7] because a corrupt president could do a great deal of damage to the nation in a short amount of time. However, he, too, had concerns about giving Congress the power to remove a president. Although he agreed

James Madison worried about the possible misuse of impeachment powers, believing that impeachment could be used as a means to manipulate a president.

that treason and bribery were serious enough to deserve impeachment, Madison objected to the use of "mal-administration" as an impeachable offense. He feared that this wording might allow a majority in Congress who disagreed with the president on certain issues to use impeachment as a threat or a tool to force the president to accept their beliefs. Mason agreed to withdraw the word, and the final version of the Constitution stated that a president could be impeached for "treason, bribery, or other high crimes and misdemeanors against the state"[8]

The Constitutional Solution

Still concerned about impeachment becoming a political fight, Madison preferred to have the Supreme Court decide the fate of the president in impeachment trials. Sherman, however, noted that this would be "improper . . . because the judges would be appointed by the president."[9] A president might be tempted to appoint judges to the Supreme Court on the condition that they support him in all impeachment attempts.

Eventually, the founders agreed on a basic procedure to follow in cases in which it is in the country's best interests to remove an unfit president from office without waiting for the next election. The House of Representatives was given the sole power to impeach the president. A simple majority of those present and voting would be all that was required to impeach. These charges would then come before the Senate, which was given the sole power to convict or acquit the president of the impeachment charges. The founders required a two-thirds majority vote to convict and remove a president from office on the

HISTORY OF IMPEACHMENT

In the entire history of the United States, only fifteen men have been impeached by the U.S. Senate. Of that number, only seven have actually been convicted—all of them federal judges. Two more, including President Nixon, resigned rather than face impeachment charges.

The first person impeached was Senator William Blount of Tennessee. Blount got himself into trouble in 1797 by hatching a bizarre plot with the British to drive the Spanish out of Florida. The Senate, however, dismissed the case on the grounds that the Constitution did not allow for the impeachment of a senator.

In 1803, the Senate convicted and removed Judge John Pickering of New Hampshire for repeated drunkenness and unlawful procedures in his courtroom. The following year, the House of Representatives brought impeachment charges against Supreme Court justice Samuel Chase. The case was basically a political fight between Thomas Jefferson's Democratic Republicans and the Federalists, of whom Chase was a member. Chase was acquitted, and no Supreme Court justice has been impeached since.

Until the twentieth century, conviction on impeachment charges was almost impossible to achieve. Following Pickering's removal from office, the only man impeached and convicted for the next 110 years was Tennessee judge West Hughes Humphreys, who was removed for joining the Confederate government in 1862.

The most active era of impeachment was the 1980s. During that decade, three federal judges—Harry Claiborne of Nevada, Alcee Hastings of Florida, and Walter Nixon of Mississippi—were impeached and convicted. Those who favored the impeachment of Bill Clinton frequently cited the Hastings and Nixon cases because perjury was one of the charges on which those two men were convicted.

grounds that removal should occur only with widespread agreement.

Grounds for Impeachment

While the Constitution clearly spelled out the procedure, it was not as clear in defining what acts were grounds for impeachment. What exactly did the Constitution mean by "other high crimes and misdemeanors"? Was this limited to obvious direct crimes such as treason, bribery, and theft of public funds, or could other violations of law be considered as undermining the laws of the republic?

In trying to explain what the Constitution meant, people such as Alexander Hamilton of New York only muddied the waters. Hamilton wrote that impeachment was "the proper remedy" for "offenses which proceed from . . . the abuse or violation of some public trust." [10] "Abuse of some public trust" is such a vague concept that it can be interpreted as anything from a minor violation of law to treason.

Johnson Makes Enemies

The impeachment clause of the Constitution went untested throughout the terms of office of the first sixteen U.S. presidents, until Andrew Johnson ran into a congressional hornet's nest. Johnson had risen from humble beginnings as a tailor to become a leading statesman during the Civil War. During that conflict, Senator Johnson had been the only member of Congress representing a Southern state who refused to join the Confederacy. He had stood firm in the face of death threats in his native Tennessee and had faced down political en-

The self-made Andrew Johnson, once dubbed "the greatest man of the age," was also the first president to be impeached.

emies and mobs with a gun. The *New York Times* called him "the greatest man of the age."[11] Abraham Lincoln was so impressed with Johnson that he asked him to run as his vice president in 1864 even though Lincoln was a Republican and Johnson a Democrat.

Johnson's good name suffered a horrible blow on Lincoln's inauguration day, however. Trying to calm his nerves before his speech by drinking liquor, Johnson accidentally overdid it. The embarrassing speech he gave in his drunken state made it difficult for many listeners to ever take him seriously again.

Shortly after Johnson took office, Lincoln was assassinated, so Johnson became president. The Republicans in Congress, who had been disappointed by Lincoln's policy of imposing few punishments and restrictions on the defeated rebels, expected Johnson to be their ally. After all, he had repeatedly called Confederates "traitors" and had been a harsh military governor of Tennessee after it fell to Union troops early in the war.

Johnson disappointed the Republicans by following Lincoln's lenient policies. Then he shocked and angered them by working to allow Southern states to rejoin the Union without reforming their racist attitudes. Many Northerners lost whatever respect they had for Johnson. Ill feelings against Johnson ran so high that crowds shouted him down when the president tried to give a public speech. In November 1867, the House Judiciary Committee voted to impeach Johnson. The House rejected the move on a vote of 108 to 57 only because no specific charges were cited.

The First Impeachment

Throughout his presidency, Johnson feuded with Secretary of War Edwin Stanton, a holdover from Lincoln's presidency. Ironically, Stanton had once praised Johnson's role as military governor of Tennessee as a "position of personal toil and danger more hazardous than was encountered by any other citizen or military officer of the United States."[12]

Stanton aggressively supported the policies of Johnson's Republican enemies, however, and was a constant thorn in Johnson's side. To protect Stanton from Johnson's displeasure,

The dismissal of Secretary of War Edwin Stanton from his post instigated Johnson's impeachment.

Congress passed the Tenure of Office Act. This law prohibited the president from firing his own cabinet officers without the approval of Congress. Many legal experts, including Stanton himself, doubted that the Constitution allowed Congress to take such powers away from the president.

Johnson soon discovered that Stanton had hidden from him a recommendation of mercy for a woman falsely accused of involvement in Lincoln's assassination. Unaware of the recommendation, Johnson had allowed the woman to be hanged. Furious, Johnson dismissed Stanton from his post. It was exactly what the Republicans had hoped the stubborn, hot-tempered president would do.

On February 24, 1868, the House voted to impeach Johnson by a vote of 126 to 47. The motion to impeach contained no specific charges, but Johnson's secretary of the navy, Gideon Welles, commented that the House "would have impeached the President for stepping on a dog's tail." [13] Only after the vote did the House draw up a list of eleven articles of impeachable acts, including violating the Tenure of Office Act. Ohio's James Ashley wanted to charge Johnson with conspiring to murder Lincoln, but the House did not include his reckless charge.

A strong majority of the public wanted the president thrown out of office. Most people expected that Johnson would resign rather than face further embarrassment in the hostile Senate. Others spread rumors that Johnson was gathering an army to fight for control of the country. But Johnson did neither. He was determined to stay at his job until Congress legally forced him out of it. That meant that the impeachment charges would have to be tried in the Senate. With no previous experience to draw on, the Senate had to figure out how to put into action the Constitution's vague and sketchy guidelines for an impeachment trial.

Setting the Ground Rules

On March 4, 1868, the Senate doors opened and the seven House representatives chosen to prosecute the case marched in by twos, arm in arm. They formally read the eleven articles of impeachment. The following day, as provided for by the Constitution, Supreme Court chief justice Salmon Chase opened the trial before a packed gallery. He swore in the senators and charged them to uphold the Constitution by judging the case fairly.

Thaddeus Stevens, the fiery leader of the House Republicans, was supposed to lead the prosecution. But he had grown weak from an illness that was to prove fatal and the task went to Benjamin Butler of Massachusetts. The arrogant Butler, a man with a shady record as a Civil War general, made clear his contempt for the president when he boasted that he and his colleagues were going to try Johnson like a horse thief.

Johnson had to pay for his five lawyers out of his own pocket. They were led by the highly respected William Evarts, a New York Republican who put aside his own personal hatred of Johnson to handle the case. Noting that the specific charges against Johnson had not been announced until the opening of the trial, the lawyers pleaded for forty days to prepare their defense. Chase gave them ten.

It quickly became clear that the normal rules of the courtroom did not apply to the Senate. Johnson's supporters pointed out that Senator Ben Wade of Ohio had a clear conflict of interest in the case. Since there was no vice president at this time, the next in line for the presidency was the president of the Senate, who was Wade. He obviously had a strong motive to vote against Johnson, regardless of the facts, so that he could achieve his ambition of becoming president. In any other trial, the judge would rule on whether Wade could remain as a juror in the case.

Johnson's impeachment trial was fraught with controversy. The president's supporters were angered by Senator Ben Wade's bias while Salmon Chase's impartiality offended Republicans.

The Republican senators, however, did not want to risk their advantage by letting an impartial judge make the rules. Chase had alarmed them with his compromise ruling allowing the president ten days to prepare the case. They had expected Chase, a fellow Republican, to side with them on all important matters. To maintain their advantage, Charles Sumner of Massachusetts moved that the chief justice had no authority to rule or vote on any matter. The Senate stopped just short of Sumner's suggestion and allowed Chase to rule on questions of evidence only. Even then, his ruling could be overruled by a simple majority vote of the senators. In other words, the majority party that controlled the prosecutors and the jury could make the rules. By this procedure, Wade was allowed to sit in judgment along with his colleagues. The Senate also overturned Chase's ruling that Johnson could call his cabinet ministers as witnesses.

President Johnson established his own tradition by refusing to appear before the Senate to answer the charges. Insisting that he would not let the Senate distract him from his duties to the country, Johnson continued at his job as if nothing unusual was happening. In reality, the government ground to a halt for nearly three months as all eyes focused on this spectacular trial.

Saved by a Single Vote

In presenting their case, the House Republicans blasted Johnson at every opportunity. Senator Sumner proclaimed, "Search history and I am sure you will find no elected ruler who, during the same short time, had done so much mischief in his country." Other Republicans warned that Johnson would destroy the nation if left in office. Representative Butler argued that the senators did not have to follow a strict interpretation of the law in this case. "You are a law unto yourselves,"[14] he said, and so they could vote to impeach for any reason they chose.

When the congressmen finished, the president's lawyers pleaded their case. They argued that the Tenure of Office Act was unconstitutional. Since Johnson had sworn an oath to protect the Constitution, he had no choice but to challenge the law. As for the articles of impeachment dealing with such things as Johnson's intemperate remarks, Johnson was entitled to speak his mind, as provided for in the Bill of Rights guarantee of free speech.

Their arguments, however, did not appear to change any minds. As the Senate gathered for the crucial roll call vote on May 16, many agreed with the *New York Times*, which declared

Butler, who encouraged senators to impeach the president for any reason they chose, reads a speech while Johnson looks on.

that conviction was all but certain. Johnson even wrote out a letter of resignation to be delivered after the vote.

However, Senator Edmund Ross of Kansas would play a vital role. His vote allowed Johnson to escape conviction by a single vote on two of the articles of impeachment. Having failed on the strongest of their charges, the Senate declined to vote on the other nine. Although the Senate either ignored or overrode nearly everything Johnson tried to do in his remaining years, the president did finish out his term.

Nixon and Watergate

Although no president has ever been impeached and convicted, Richard Nixon avoided that fate only by resigning. Nixon, who was elected president in 1968, was obsessed with opponents who criticized his Vietnam War policies. Some of his supporters viewed these opponents as traitors and believed that this justified using questionable and even illegal tactics against them. During the presidential campaign of 1972, a group of Nixon's campaign workers were caught breaking into the office of the national Democratic Party chairman at the Watergate building in Washington, D.C., in an attempt to bug his phone.

Nixon did not approve or even know about the Watergate break-in plans. But when he found out who was responsible, he made the mistake of trying to protect the burglars and cover up the connection between them and his campaign organization. Furthermore, he had secretly taped all of his conversations in the White House, which provided investigators with proof of his conspiracy to obstruct justice.

The case against Nixon appeared to be so strong that the Senate began establishing rules for the coming impeachment trial. Among the rules was that senators could not directly question anyone or offer any motions during the trial. All questions or motions had to be written down and handed to the presiding officer.

The trial never came about, however. Senator Barry Goldwater of Arizona visited Nixon and informed him that few of his fellow Republicans would support him. In fact, the president

EDMUND ROSS: THE MAN WHO SAVED JOHNSON

Edmund Ross never imagined he would find himself in the eye of a national political hurricane. A man with no political experience or ambitions, he had been appointed to his Senate post only two years earlier to fill the vacancy left by James Lane, who had committed suicide. As the impeachment trial of Andrew Johnson neared its end, however, all eyes were on Ross. When the Republicans counted the votes, they found themselves one vote short of the two-thirds majority needed to convict the president. Ross was the only senator left who had refused to indicate how he would vote on the charges.

There were signs that he would vote with the Republicans, as he had done on virtually all issues. He was a Republican himself and had fought for the North in the Civil War. Ross had little respect for President Johnson as a person, and he disagreed with most of his policies. But Ross's stubborn silence during the impeachment trial drove people on both sides of the issue nearly mad.

Worried that Ross might desert his party, Republicans tried every tactic they could think of to pressure him into convicting Johnson. They hired a detective to keep an eye on his residence. Mysterious men threatened his girlfriend. Party leaders warned Ross that he would be investigated for bribery if he did not vote to convict. Kansas voters flooded his office with telegrams demanding he vote against Johnson.

But Ross refused to be intimidated. In a reply to one blustery telegram, he wrote, "I do not recognize your right to demand that I shall vote either for or against conviction. I have taken an oath to do impartial justice."

As the roll call vote on Article 11 of the impeachment charges was called on May 16, 1868, not one senator knew how Ross would vote. Halfway through the voting, it became obvious that he would be the deciding vote. The Republicans had thirty-five certain votes and needed only one more to convict.

Ross later admitted that he was not certain of his decision until a few days before the vote. But when his turn came, he declared without hesitation, "Not guilty." He claimed that he feared the results of partisan rule and the possible damage to the office of the president more than he feared the waning power of Johnson or the loss of his Senate seat. In the end, he decided to give the country the benefit of the doubt. By that slim margin was Johnson's presidency saved.

Ross was well aware that he was sacrificing his career and his reputation by voting as he did. When he returned to Kansas, he was scorned as a traitor and physically beaten. Neither he nor any of the other six Republicans who voted against conviction were ever re-elected to the Senate.

could count on the support of only eighteen of the one hundred senators. Seeing that his cause was hopeless, Nixon resigned the presidency.

The Independent Counsel Law

The Watergate turmoil generated concern about the U.S. Justice Department's ability to investigate charges of corruption in the executive branch of the government. Since the Justice Department is part of the executive branch, its top officials are appointed by the president, which posed the problem. At one point in the Watergate affair, the Justice Department's chief investigator began to zero in on evidence of Nixon's wrongdoing and Nixon promptly fired him.

This act outraged the public. It was clear evidence of a major flaw in the system. How could the executive branch of government be trusted to investigate itself? In response to this concern, Congress passed a law authorizing the Office of the Independent Counsel. The independent counsel would be appointed by a panel of judges and would be charged with the

President Richard Nixon chose to resign from office rather than face impeachment. Here, Nixon is shown giving a farewell speech to the public.

SATURDAY NIGHT MASSACRE

John Dean, a White House lawyer at the time of the Watergate scandal, described Kenneth Starr's investigation as "Richard Nixon's last revenge." He was referring to Nixon's infamous "Saturday Night Massacre" that prompted the creation of the Office of the Independent Counsel.

When evidence that federal officials might be involved in the Watergate cover-up began to surface, worries about a conflict of interest began to arise.

How could the federal investigators be trusted to investigate wrongdoing in their own administration? It would be easy for them to overlook or hide the truth to protect themselves, their bosses, and their friends.

In response to these fears, Attorney General Elliot Richardson created the Office of the Watergate Special Prosecution Force on May 31, 1973. He promised that this investigative force, led by Archibald Cox, would be independent of the Justice Department and would have full authority to conduct the investigation.

But when Cox pursued the case aggressively and closed in on evidence of Nixon's involvement, the president was furious. On Saturday evening on October 20, 1973, he ordered Richardson to fire Cox. Richardson was stunned. The president had no business interfering with this independent investigation. Rather than carry out what he believed to be an illegal order, Richardson submitted his resignation.

Nixon then told Deputy Attorney General William Ruckelshaus to fire Cox. Ruckelshaus also resigned rather than obey the order. Finally, Nixon called Solicitor General Robert Bork, who agreed to dismiss Cox. Later that night, White House press secretary Ron Ziegler announced that the president had eliminated the Watergate Special Prosecution Force.

Nixon's actions so outraged the public that lawmakers began the impeachment inquiry that eventually led to his resignation. The Saturday Night Massacre also provided convincing evidence that the federal government could not be trusted to investigate itself. It led Congress to create the Office of the Independent Counsel, giving it broad powers to investigate wrongdoing.

responsibility of investigating charges of wrongdoing in the executive branch.

It was the creation of this independent counsel that started the chain of legal events that led to the impeachment of Bill Clinton.

Chapter 2

The Crime

IN THE SUMMER of 1994, reporters began probing into a com-
plicated real estate venture in Arkansas. There appeared to be
a number of shady dealings in a land development known as
Whitewater that caused a number of investors to lose a great deal
of money. The people involved in this venture included several
friends of the Clintons and the law firm for whom Hillary Clinton worked. Questions soon arose about whether the president
or first lady had been involved in any criminal activity.

Frustrated by the negative attention the case was getting, President Clinton invited the independent counsel to investigate the
matter and get all the facts out
in the open. In August 1994, Independent Counsel Kenneth
Starr began his official probe of
the Whitewater case.

The investigation dragged
on for several years as Starr
sought to untangle the complex financial arrangements of
Whitewater. During this time,
he did uncover enough evidence of criminal activity to

*Independent Counsel Kenneth Starr
was invited by Clinton to investigate
the Whitewater scandal.*

bring charges of fraud against several friends and associates of the Clintons. A couple of these associates hinted that the Clintons were somehow involved in some of this criminal activity. Starr suspected that people were hiding the truth and tried to get witnesses to testify against the Clintons. But he could not find evidence that could be used to charge either of them with a crime.

Enter Paula Jones

At about the same time that the Whitewater investigation began, Clinton's political enemies attacked him from another angle. For years, stories had been circulating about Clinton's sexual affairs. One of these stories had nearly ruined Clinton's presidential bid during the primaries of the 1992 election. The president's opponents were furious that people did not seem to be taking these accounts seriously. In their view, the incidents were proof that Clinton was not morally fit to be president.

One of those opponents was Clint Jackson, a lawyer from Little Rock, Arkansas, who had been a bitter enemy of Clinton's in Arkansas politics for years. Since Clinton's rise in national politics, Jackson had been scouring the state for proof of Clinton's sexual misconduct. By 1994, he had managed to collect enough evidence to persuade two reporters to look into his charges. The reporters then wrote articles detailing claims that, while Clinton was governor, he used state troopers to secretly bring young women to him.

A former Arkansas government employee named Paula Jones read one of these articles, which related a story by Arkansas trooper Danny Ferguson. Ferguson claimed to have brought a young woman named Paula to a hotel room in Little Rock in which Clinton was staying.

According to Jones, she recognized the incident as one that she had been involved in in May 1991. Although she had refused the president's advances and nothing more had come of the situation, Jones believed that she now needed to protect her reputation. Jones wanted to sue the president for sexual harassment.

Some conservative activists put her in touch with Virginia lawyer Gil Davis and his associate, Joe Cammarata, who agreed

Originally only asking for a $25,000 settlement, Paula Jones (left) filed a $700,000 lawsuit in 1994 when Clinton failed to apologize to the former government employee.

to take on her case. Originally, Jones wanted only a $25,000 settlement and a private apology from the president. Clinton, however, refused to apologize, insisting that he could not recall meeting Jones and that he had done nothing wrong. When Jones filed the suit in 1994, she instead asked for $700,000. She claimed that Clinton had used his power as governor to violate her civil rights, and, according to Jones, she was denied promotion in her government job after the incident and she suffered emotional distress.

Can a President Be Sued?

The lawsuit brought up a new and controversial legal issue. Never before had a president been sued while in office for something that allegedly occurred before he became president. Was this legal?

Clinton did not think that the Constitution allowed for such a suit, and his lawyers sought to delay the case until Clinton's term of office ended. They pointed out that the president had enormous responsibilities to the nation and that, if the courts allowed the lawsuit to go forward, what would prevent attention seekers of all kinds from filing lawsuits against a president? How could a president do his job if he were constantly being bombarded with lawsuits that might have no merit?

The president's lawyers took this argument all the way to the Supreme Court. But in May 1997, the nation's highest court ruled unanimously that a sitting president can be sued for actions outside his official duties. In its opinion, such a case would not occupy much of the president's time and attention. The only concession the court made to the president was that the trial

WHY PAULA JONES SUED THE PRESIDENT

The spark that lit the fuse on Clinton's impeachment happened seven and a half years before the actual Senate trial. On March 11, 1991, Paula Rosalee Corbin began working at a low-paying job for a state agency known as the Arkansas Industrial Development Commission. She had had the job for less than two months when she was assigned to work the reception desk at the Governor's Quality Management Conference at the Excelsior Hotel in Little Rock. The governor in charge of the conference was Bill Clinton.

According to Corbin (who became Paula Jones when she married in December of that year), state trooper Danny Ferguson approached her at about 2:30 P.M. on May 8, 1991, and gave her a slip of paper with the governor's room number on it. Ferguson said Clinton wanted to see her. Jones went to the room, where she refused a sexual advance from Clinton.

Jones says she did not report the incident for fear of losing her job. But she appeared to suffer no hardship from her refusal and received regular pay increases.

She quit her job early in 1993 and moved to California with her husband. Her story might never have come to light were it not for an article in the *American Spectator* in 1994. A friend read the article to Jones while she was back in Arkansas on a visit later that year. The article quoted a state trooper as saying that a woman named Paula had told him she was willing to be Clinton's girlfriend. Upset because the article made it appear that she made herself available for an affair with Clinton, Jones initially asked only for an apology from the president.

When Clinton refused to even acknowledge that he had ever met her, Jones went to court. From there, the dominoes kept falling until Clinton was impeached.

Clinton did not favor settling with Jones out of court because he believed that she did not have a strong case.

judge, when making decisions in the case, would need to take into account the unusual responsibilities of a president and not cause him needless distractions that could harm the nation.

A Settlement?

Lawyers for both sides tried to arrange a settlement out of court, but neither the Clintons nor Paula Jones favored the idea. The Clintons believed that Jones had a very weak case. Even if her story were true and Clinton had made a pass at her, that was not sexual harassment. She had never been pressured any further and was neither fired nor demoted in her job. Furthermore, while Trooper Ferguson's testimony backed Jones's in saying that the incident took place, his account differed dramatically from hers. According to Ferguson, Jones approached him after the hotel room meeting and offered to be the governor's girl-friend.

Nevertheless, the president did not want to go through the potentially embarrassing testimony of a trial during his presidency. His lawyers offered Jones the money she was asking, $700,000, to drop the case. Her lawyers strongly advised she take it. But Jones refused unless an apology from the president was part of the deal. That the president would not do. Unable to get Jones to change her mind even after early rulings by Judge Susan Webber Wright weakened their case, attorneys Davis and Cammarata resigned in frustration.

Up until this point, Clinton seemed to have eluded his opponents. Ken Starr had found no substantial evidence of criminal wrongdoing on Clinton's part in the Whitewater case and the Jones lawsuit appeared to be shaky at best.

But Jones eventually found another group of lawyers willing to press her case, and the trial moved forward. To Clinton's dismay, Judge Wright did not heed the Supreme Court's suggestion that she could limit the scope of the testimony out of respect for the president's unique position. She allowed Jones's lawyers to range far beyond the facts of the immediate case to look into the president's past and present for any evidence that might portray him as a sexual harasser.

Rulings by Judge Susan Webber Wright (pictured) showed no favoritism to any of the parties involved in the litigation.

An Unexpected Twist

While Jones's lawyers were preparing their case, they heard an incredible story from a woman named Linda Tripp. Tripp had struck up a friendship with a new coworker at the Pentagon named Monica Lewinsky. Both Tripp and Lewinsky had also worked for a time in the Clinton White House. As the two became close, Lewinsky confided a shocking secret to Tripp. While working as a White House intern, she had begun an affair with the president.

Lewinsky (bottom) at first was reluctant to harm the president's reputation. Tripp (top) recorded her conversations with Lewinsky in order to obtain proof of the affair.

In the fall of 1997, Tripp began secretly tape-recording phone conversations with Lewinsky. Her motives for doing so have been hotly debated. Tripp argued that the Paula Jones investigation into the president's sexual life put her in an impossible position. Because of Lewinsky's confessions to her, she knew things about the president that Clinton would not want to be made public. With the power of the presidency at his disposal, Clinton could put great pressure on people to cover up the truth. Lewinsky was insisting that she would lie to protect the president. If Tripp were questioned on the matter, she would face a choice of telling the truth and having no one believe her or lying and possibly facing charges of perjury. To protect herself, she claimed, she recorded the conversations with Lewinsky as proof that the affair really took place.

Tripp's critics, however, argue that the recordings were not only a vicious betrayal of a friend but an attempt by Clinton's enemies to entrap the president. Tripp made the tapes at the suggestion of a

MONICA LEWINSKY

The young woman at the center of the Clinton scandal was a dark-haired, insecure Californian named Monica Lewinsky. Monica was born in San Francisco in 1973 to Bernard and Marcia Lewinsky. Bernard was a successful medical doctor, and he lavished his wealth upon his family. Monica grew up with younger brother Michael in a million-dollar house in Beverly Hills and graduated from Bel Air Prep School. Money did not buy security and happiness, however. Lewinsky's father paid little attention to her, and he and his wife split in a messy divorce in 1988.

Lewinsky attended Santa Monica Junior College for two years. There she began an affair with her drama teacher, which continued when she moved on to Lewis and Clark College in Oregon. She graduated from the school in 1995 with a degree in psychology.

A family friend who had influence with the Clinton administration soon got her a job as a White House intern in the Office of Legislative Affairs. Lewinsky moved to Washington, D.C., to share an apartment with her mother, ironically in the Watergate complex, in which Nixon's impeachment problems had begun.

At the White House, she found herself attracted to Clinton, who returned her flirting. When White House staff noticed she was becoming too familiar with the president, she was transferred to the public affairs office of the Pentagon. But rather than sending her out of harm's way, the move put her into close contact with Linda Tripp, who drew Lewinsky in to reveal her secrets and then exposed them to prosecutors.

Threatened with a twenty-seven-year jail sentence if she did not cooperate with Ken Starr's investigation, Lewinsky considered suicide. Eventually her lawyers arranged a deal with Starr, and she reluctantly told her story to the world.

The graphic details included in the Starr report infuriated Lewinsky. "As a result of the report, I felt very violated," she said. In her testimony, she steadfastly refused to give Starr what he wanted—evidence that Clinton told her to lie in her Paula Jones affidavit.

When the impeachment was over, Lewinsky expressed some remorse over her actions. "I wouldn't dream of asking Chelsea [the president's daughter] and Mrs. Clinton to forgive me," she told an interviewer. "But I would ask them to know that I'm sorry for what happened and for what they've been through."

friend, literary agent Lucianne Goldberg, who openly despised Clinton. Furthermore, critics said that Tripp did not use her recordings in self-defense but sought out Jones's lawyers so that they could put Clinton in an awkward bind.

Judge Wright had said that Jones's lawyers could bring in evidence of the president's past sexual activity to establish a pattern of sexual harassment. That meant they could question Clinton and Lewinsky about the affair, leaving the president with the choice of either admitting to a shocking, shameful affair with Lewinsky or lying about it under oath.

The Independent Counsel Gets Involved

The Jones lawyers also issued a subpoena, or order to testify, to Monica Lewinsky. Unaware that Tripp had secretly recorded their conversations, Lewinsky thought she could safely deny the affair with Clinton. After all, she and Clinton were the only ones who had any actual knowledge about their actions. On January 7, Lewinsky submitted an affidavit in which she swore that she did not have an affair with the president.

Armed with a tape recording that contradicted her testimony, however, Jones's lawyers had strong evidence that Lewinsky had

Capitol Hill personnel sort through the Tripp tapes. These tapes contradict the affidavit that Lewinsky submitted on January 7.

lied under oath. Tripp's taped conversations further hinted that Lewinsky and the president had talked about how to deny the affair. If this was true, the president could be guilty of obstructing justice and tampering with a witness. In addition, Clinton was scheduled to answer questions from Jones's lawyers under oath on January 17. Based on Lewinsky's false affidavit, Jones's lawyers thought that there was a good chance that the president was going to lie under oath as well.

Lying under oath, tampering with witnesses, and obstructing justice are all criminal charges—the type of wrongdoing that Ken Starr's investigation had been pursuing against Clinton without success for more than three years. Just as the Whitewater investigation was finally fizzling, Jones's lawyers alerted Starr to the new developments.

The accusations against Clinton and Lewinsky had nothing to do with Starr's Whitewater investigation or with any of the other matters that Starr had been assigned to investigate. But according to the independent counsel law, he had a duty to "advise the House of Representatives of any substantial and credible information . . . that may constitute grounds for impeachment." [15] Charges that the president might have urged Lewinsky to lie under oath and that he was about to lie under oath himself seemed to fall under that category. Starr asked Attorney General Janet Reno for the authority to expand his probe into the Lewinsky affair. After seeing the evidence, Reno granted his request.

Starr Zeros In

Although Tripp's tapes were strong evidence that Clinton may have been involved in violations of the law, they would not be enough by themselves to convict him. Starr needed Lewinsky's cooperation in order to make the charges stick. He and his investigators surprised Lewinsky at a lunch with Tripp and took Lewinsky to a hotel room for questioning. There she learned about Tripp's betrayal of confidence. Lewinsky's own words on the tapes indicated that she had lied in a sworn statement to the court. For nearly ten hours, investigators questioned, pleaded for cooperation, and threatened Lewinsky with jail for perjury for

LINDA TRIPP: SHE SPILLED THE SECRET

Starr would never have gotten involved in the Paula Jones–Monica Lewinsky matter if not for Linda Rose Tripp. Tripp and Lewinsky were unlikely friends. The forty-eight-year-old Tripp was a divorced mother with children nearly Lewinsky's age.

Nevertheless, Lewinsky began confiding in Tripp shortly after Vernon Jordan helped find her a job at the Pentagon. Not only did Tripp appear to be a good listener, but she had been working at the White House when Lewinsky arrived there to start her job as an intern. She was familiar with many of the inner workings of the White House that Lewinsky described.

While Tripp had sympathy for Lewinsky's tale of frustrated love in the White House, she had none for the Clinton administration. She had originally come to the White House to work for George Bush's administration but was allowed to stay on after Clinton took office. Eventually, though, Tripp's attitude worried her superiors. A Bush adviser described Tripp as a person with "a chip on her shoulder" who relished controversy. When she publicly referred to White House lawyers as "the Three Stooges," White House officials decided she needed to be moved out. In August 1994 she was transferred to the Pentagon, where she worked at an $88,000 a year job until the time the Lewinsky scandal broke.

In the fall of 1997, she began taping her private conversations with Lewinsky. These conversations included several discussions about how Lewinsky could deny having a relationship with the president. Although such taping without the other party's consent was illegal, those tapes provided devastating evidence that both Lewinsky and the president lied under oath in their depositions.

Tripp claimed she taped the conversations only so that others could not charge her with lying if she was forced to testify against Clinton. The American public, however, strongly disapproved of her manipulation of Lewinsky, calling it a betrayal of a friend's confidence. William Ginsburg, Lewinsky's first attorney in the case, commented, "Linda Tripp ought to be in jail for violating Monica Lewinsky's privacy."

her affidavit in the Jones case. This set off a long, tense, and often bitter negotiation between Lewinsky's lawyer and the prosecutors over an offer of immunity from prosecution, which would dismiss all possible charges against her in exchange for her cooperation.

Meanwhile, on January 17, 1998, Clinton gave his testimony in the Jones case. Under oath, he said that he could not recall ever meeting Jones and that he certainly had never sexually harassed her. When the questioning turned to Monica Lewinsky, Clinton was clearly surprised by what Jones's lawyers knew. Nevertheless, he claimed that he could not remember any time when he and Lewinsky might have been alone together, much less had any sexual relations.

The Denial

Within a few days, the shocking claims of Clinton's alleged affair with a young White House intern were spreading throughout the country. Clinton strongly denied the rumors. At one point, he wagged his finger into the television cameras and stated flatly, "I did not have sexual relations with that woman, Miss Lewinsky." [16] He promised reporters that he would cooperate fully with any investigation into the matter and would see to it that the country got all the information on the case as soon as possible.

Hillary Clinton rushed to her husband's defense, dismissing the stories about Lewinsky as part of an elaborate campaign to destroy the president by "a politically motivated prosecutor who

Clinton publicly denied having an affair with Lewinsky, stating on television that he "did not have sexual relations with that woman, Miss Lewinsky."

is allied with right-wing opponents of my husband."[17] Clinton's supporters rallied behind him. Most of them were convinced that the president could not have been so reckless that he would have carried on an affair while he was the target of a sexual harassment suit and other sexual misconduct claims.

But despite widespread public criticism, Starr focused his investigation on the Clinton-Lewinsky affair. For months, he called a steady stream of witnesses before a grand jury, including White House aides, Secret Service agents, and even Lewinsky's mother.

The Confession

All through the spring and into the summer of 1998, rumors floated about what had happened between Clinton and Lewinsky. For a time it appeared that the matter would never be fully resolved. As long as Lewinsky did not cooperate, Starr had no case against the president. Even if she did admit to an affair, the president could deny it and it would be one person's word against another's.

A break in the case came when Lewinsky switched lawyers. Her new attorneys persuaded her to look after her own interests. During the summer, they struck a deal with the independent counsel that would grant Lewinsky immunity from prosecution. In exchange, Lewinsky provided Starr's investigators with a detailed report of her affair with Clinton. Some of her testimony directly contradicted the president's. Whereas Clinton claimed he could not recall any occasions in which he and Lewinsky were alone in the Oval Office of the White House, Lewinsky described eight such encounters. Furthermore, she was able to produce a dress that was spotted with the president's semen from one sexual encounter.

Faced with this evidence, Clinton finally came forward in a nationally televised address to admit that he had had an inappropriate relationship with Lewinsky. Clinton also apologized for misleading the nation with his earlier denials.

At about the same time, Starr summoned Clinton to appear before the grand jury that was meeting to consider criminal charges in the matter.

Chapter 3

Punishing the President

THE TONE OF Clinton's public remarks infuriated many people. In his speech, Clinton put much of the blame for the current situation on Starr for prying into private matters in an attempt to embarrass him. Instead of coming clean with a full confession, Clinton hedged at every step. His description of his relationship with Lewinsky as "inappropriate" fell far short of admitting that it was sexual in nature, and his admission that he had misled the public fell far short of confessing that he had lied outright to the American people.

Of even more concern to the president was the reaction of his supporters, many of whom had publicly defended him against claims of his affair with Lewinsky. Clinton's confession stunned them. Many reacted angrily at having been duped. For the first time, the solid support that Clinton had enjoyed in opinion polls began to crack.

Now that the president's wrongdoing was exposed, the question was what to do about it. More than a hundred newspaper editorials across the country asked Clinton to resign. The question of impeachment was seriously raised, not just by Clinton opponents, but even by Democratic senator Joseph Lieberman of Connecticut, a longtime friend and ally of Clinton. An impassioned supporter of strong moral values, Lieberman felt that Clinton had disgraced his office and should be called into account for his actions. The debate arose: Were Clinton's mistakes impeachable actions or were they private sins that did not affect his ability to perform the job to which he had been elected?

Impeachment Inquiry

Ken Starr believed that the president had committed many impeachable offenses. On September 10, he sent his report to Congress with thirty-six boxes of evidence to support his charges, including transcripts of Clinton's videotaped testimony to the grand jury.

The House of Representatives is a large body made up of 435 members. Rather than bringing all business for consideration before all the members, the House assigns various committees the task of recommending which issues within their assigned area should come before the full House. Impeachment matters fell under the control of the Judiciary Committee, chaired by Representative Henry Hyde of Illinois. Hyde noted that history taught that impeachment could succeed only if it re-

Representative Henry Hyde of Illinois is shown here speaking in front of Starr's 36 boxes of evidence. As chairman of the Judiciary Committee, impeachment matters fell under his committee's control.

ceived bipartisan support—the support of both Republicans and Democrats. Johnson's impeachment had failed primarily because it became a political battle between rival parties. Nixon had been in no danger of impeachment until the evidence persuaded Republicans to join Democrats in supporting the president's removal. When the Starr report arrived at the House, both parties initially called for a cautious pursuit of the facts. On September 30, the Democrats joined the Republicans in authorizing an inquiry into the impeachment charges.

Behind the scenes, however, political battles were igniting. One Republican Party official rejoiced over the damage that Clinton's blunders would do to the Democrats. "This is the beginning of a permanent Republican majority,"[18] he gloated. On the other side, Clinton sympathizers began digging up dirt on some of the Republicans who would be sitting in judgment of the president's sins. They exposed the fact that Henry Hyde had once had an affair with a married woman and suggested that he was in no position to criticize the president's actions.

The Grand Jury Tapes

President Clinton seemed to be in such a weak position that his legal team was unable to prevent the Republican-dominated House from releasing the entire transcript of the Office of Independent Counsel's report without editing it, censoring any of the sexually graphic material, or even allowing the president's lawyers to first review it. In fact, most of the representatives approved the release of Starr's report before they had even read what was in it. Furthermore, against the protests of Democrats, they approved the release of the tape recording of the president's grand jury testimony to the news media. Television stations played the tapes, and Internet sources posted the Starr report with all its crude details.

The report and the grand jury tapes publicly humiliated Clinton by broadcasting his sexual activities to the entire nation. The four hours of taped testimony also caught Clinton hedging, misleading, and, according to most opinion polls, lying under oath before a grand jury.

But the effect on public opinion was the opposite of what most of those in Congress expected. The House's public airing of such private and sensitive material offended many people. Many of the juiciest details seemed to have no relevance to the case and appeared to be included only to embarrass the president. The most striking image to come out of the videotape was the sight of a battery of prosecutors relentlessly badgering a humiliated president. It generated more sympathy for a man caught in an awkward situation than anger at a president caught violating the law. The airing of the videotape of Clinton's grand jury testimony gave credibility to Clinton supporters who claimed that the entire Starr investigation had been a political power play to entrap and destroy the president.

Backlash Against the Republicans

The Republicans, said reporter Elise Ackerman, were "stunned and chastened by the negative public reaction"[19] to the release

Starr, seen here holding up the report that many felt was a partisan attack against the president, was heavily criticized for his investigation.

WHAT IS A GRAND JURY?

Although its name may seem to indicate that a grand jury is more important than an ordinary jury, a grand jury simply refers to the number of members. The usual trial jury is made up of twelve, or occasionally six, individuals. Grand juries may run from twelve to twenty-three members depending on the state.

Grand juries also differ from trial juries in other ways. Unlike a regular jury that meets in open court, a grand jury often meets secretly. The grand jury is a safeguard to protect Americans from the cost and anguish of vindictive or petty accusations. It functions as a sort of screening committee to decide if there is any reasonable basis for accusing a person of a crime. Because of this, testimony before a grand jury is generally sealed so that charges that prove to be unfounded are not brought out in the open.

The grand jury does not use the standard that a person is innocent unless proven guilty beyond a reasonable doubt. They merely determine whether the prosecution has good reason to be suspicious of a person's guilt. As a result, in a typical grand jury hearing, the prosecution presents evidence, but the other side seldom offers a complete defense.

of the report and the videotape. Democratic legislators were recharged by Democratic voters who were infuriated by the release of the report and the president's grand jury testimony. Encouraged by new public polls that showed strong support for Clinton's staying on as president and strong disapproval of the Republicans' handling of the impeachment inquiry, they went on the attack. While no one approved of Clinton's behavior in this matter, Democrats argued that his opponents were even worse. They painted Starr as a prosecutor out of control, a man so obsessed with getting Clinton that he poured $40 million of the taxpayers' money into an investigation of what was essentially a private affair that was none of his business.

Both parties anxiously awaited the results of the 1998 congressional election in the first week of November. Before the grand jury videotape disaster, Republicans had been confident that they would turn Clinton's misdeeds into large gains in both the House and the Senate. Many had been running televised ads that tried to feed on voter distrust of Clinton. But on the eve of

(Top) Besieged by the media, Kenneth Starr gives a speech outside his Washington office. (Bottom) Newt Gingrich resigned his seat in the House of Representatives in response to public scorn over his handling of the impeachment matter.

the elections, public outcry over the Republicans' handling of the situation had shrunk their hopes to a gain of a half dozen or so seats in the House and a couple in the Senate.

The reality proved even worse. The Republicans gained no seats in the Senate and actually lost in the House. The U.S. voters had issued a stinging rebuke to those Republicans who had tried to make an issue of impeaching Clinton. The Republican leader in the House of Representatives, Newt Gingrich of Georgia, resigned his seat in response to criticism concerning his handling of the impeachment matter. He was replaced by Bob Livingston of Louisiana, who declared that he would like to see the whole impeachment matter finished by the end of the year.

It appeared to virtually all observers that Bill Clinton was now safe from impeachment. As Republican Lindsay Graham of South Carolina noted, "The president may have committed perjury, but impeachment cannot proceed without public outcry." [20]

The only public outcry was for members of Congress and the media to end the sad, sordid scandal and get on with more pressing matters.

NEWT GINGRICH: IRONIC VICTIM

The Clinton-Lewinsky scandal put Bill Clinton's presidency in grave danger. Logically, that should have strengthened the hand of Clinton's chief adversary, Newt Gingrich. Ironically, it was Gingrich who fell victim to the fallout from the affair.

Gingrich was born in 1943 and soon after was adopted by his mother's second husband, who was a career army officer. Gingrich spent his childhood at army base schools in Kansas, France, and West Germany. At the age of sixteen, his family moved to Columbus, Georgia, where Gingrich was bitten with a sense of destiny. He declared that he would one day run for Congress and try to change the course of American politics.

Gingrich married his high school math teacher, who was seven years older than he, and studied modern European history in college. After receiving his Ph.D., he began teaching history at West Georgia College in 1971.

In 1974, he made good on his teenage promise and ran for Congress. He lost but ran again two years later and was successful. Bold, brash, and eager for combat with those who disagreed with him, he irritated both Democrats and Republicans for many years. In 1987, Gingrich launched a one-man crusade against House Speaker Jim Wright of Texas. When he managed to turn up enough evidence of ethics violations to drive Wright from office, political pros realized they had to take him seriously.

Gingrich became the leader of the House Republicans. In 1994, he devised a strategy called the "Contract with America," which laid out specific actions that Republicans promised to take if elected. The Republicans won a smashing victory in the elections that November, gaining control of the House of Representatives and the Senate for the first time in half a century. Gingrich, the new Speaker of the House, proclaimed the beginning of a Republican revolution in government.

The revolution fizzled, however, as the Republican majority dwindled in 1996. Gingrich's abrasive style became a negative factor. Americans blamed him for the shutdown of the federal government during a budget dispute between Congress and the Clinton administration.

Gingrich hoped the 1998 elections would jump-start the stalled Republican revolution. Clinton's problems seemed to offer him a golden opportunity to gain congressional seats. But Gingrich's strategy of focusing on the impeachment inquiry instead of offering policies backfired. The Republicans actually lost seats, and Gingrich took the heat for the disaster. Shortly after the election, he not only gave up his position as speaker of the House but resigned his seat in Congress.

Going Through the Motions

Further events in November seemed to shovel more dirt on the grave of the impeachment effort. Ken Starr appeared before the House Judiciary Committee to defend his report. Although he came across on television as more calm and reasonable than the image that he had been branded with, he also opened himself up to more charges that he was out to get the president. After Starr's appearance, his own ethics adviser, Sam Dash, resigned in protest. According to Dash, Starr's arguments before the committee crossed the line of professional conduct. Instead of simply presenting the evidence and letting Congress draw its conclusions, Starr had become an "aggressive advocate for impeachment." [21]

Furthermore, the Paula Jones case that started the whole impeachment crisis was becoming increasingly irrelevant. First of all, Judge Wright had dismissed the case for lack of evidence. Then, in November, Jones agreed to drop her appeals of Wright's decision in exchange for $850,000. That meant that the main charge against Clinton was lying about sex in a case that a judge declared

Kenneth Starr's ethics adviser, Sam Dash, felt that the prosecutor's methods were too aggressive.

should not have come to trial in the first place and would now never come to trial. To the vast majority of Americans, that seemed like a very trivial reason to throw out an otherwise popular president. Moderate Republicans such as Christopher Shays of Connecticut were moved to say of the impeachment charges, "They wouldn't have my vote. These offenses are subimpeachable." [22]

Faced with overwhelming public disapproval of their actions, even many of Clinton's most bitter critics had to back off. In November 1998, *U.S. News & World Report* commented,

"Fewer and fewer in the GOP [Republican Party], it seems, have the stomach for impeachment any more." [23] Henry Hyde promised to bring the impeachment process to a speedy conclusion. His Judiciary Committee decided not to follow the example of the committee in the Watergate affair, which had carried on its own intense investigation of the charges against Nixon. Instead, it would rely completely on the material in Starr's report and would not even call any witnesses other than Starr, thereby being done with the matter by the end of the year.

Although impeachment now seemed unlikely, the Democrats were concerned that the public might view their opposition to impeachment as essentially saying that they thought lying under oath was acceptable. To combat this, they pressed for a resolution of censure such as the one offered by Republican representative Peter King of New York. The censure would be a simple, strongly worded statement that the Congress condemned the behavior of the president in carrying on an affair in the White House and lying about it under oath. King's version of the censure resolution included a requirement that Clinton acknowledge he was wrong and the payment of a fine.

Hyde and others, however, refused to allow any censure resolutions to come to a vote. According to them, the Constitution did not allow Congress to pass any resolutions of censure. They considered this just an easy way of avoiding the impeachment process that the Constitution demanded.

The Momentum Shifts

In the bleak days of early autumn, when impeachment seemed likely, President Clinton had been willing to accept censure and possibly other punishments, such as a fine, if the impeachment case would be dropped. Once the election results boosted his political standing, however, he abandoned his meek stance. When the House Judiciary Committee sent Clinton a list of eighty-one questions relating to impeachment issues, the president made only a token effort to cooperate. His answers to the questions were evasive, uninformative, and phrased in legal language that made it difficult to pin down exactly what he was saying. To

Members of the Judiciary Committee attentively watch Clinton's address to the nation.

many congressmen, Clinton still appeared to be denying that he had done anything wrong.

Whereas the release of Clinton's grand jury testimony had thrown water on the flames of impeachment, Clinton's uncooperative answers rekindled the fire. He claimed that his answers to Paula Jones's lawyers and to Starr's grand jury were neither false nor misleading. Seventeen times he answered that he was not certain of events or could not recall them. "His answers to the 81 questions were outrageous," complained Christopher Shays. "I mean, he still doesn't get it. He still doesn't tell the truth." [24]

Democratic representative Lee Hamilton of Indiana conceded that Clinton's responses were a disaster. "Those answers set us back with moderate Republicans," [25] said Hamilton. Many Republicans who had been inclined to let the impeachment drive die were so infuriated by what they saw as Clinton's arrogance that they became committed to following through with impeachment. No matter what the cost, no matter how many Americans wanted the issue closed, they were determined to make Clinton accountable for his actions.

The Great Divide

By this time, the partisan cooperation between parties that Hyde had said was necessary for impeachment was quickly evaporating. The Democrats' stand against impeachment was hardened by solid opinion polls that showed Americans wanted the impeachment process stopped. The Republicans' stand in favor of impeachment was hardened by their anger and disgust with Clinton.

Hyde made matters worse by proposing to expand the impeachment inquiry into new areas such as concerns about questionable fund-raising tactics used by the Clinton campaign in the last election. The senior Democrat on the House Judiciary Committee, John Conyers of Michigan, pounced on the effort. It seemed to him that Hyde was trying to do exactly what Starr had done: investigate Clinton for every little suspicion in the hopes of finding some dirt. "It's very clear that this is a partisan witch hunt that he's determined to ram through as quickly as he can," [26] Conyers scoffed.

John Conyers of Michigan came to Clinton's aid, denouncing Republicans for their partisan impeachment inquiries.

KEN STARR: THE RELENTLESS PROSECUTOR

The harder Kenneth Starr worked at his job, the more his reputation suffered. While his supporters praised him as honest and thorough, his opponents called him a prosecutor who had gone out of control.

Starr was born in 1946 in Vernon, Texas, the son of a Church of Christ minister. He grew up as an extremely serious and organized child in San Antonio. His mother remarked that, by the time he got to junior high, his hobby was polishing shoes.

Starr attended George Washington University and received his law degree from Duke University. After working as a clerk for Supreme Court chief justice Warren Burger, he went into law practice with the firm of William French Smith. When President Ronald Reagan chose Smith as his attorney general, Starr followed Smith into Washington politics. In 1983 Reagan appointed Starr to a seat on the U.S. Court of Appeals in Washington, D.C. Six years later, he accepted George Bush's offer to be solicitor general, the person responsible for arguing the administration's position before the Supreme Court. Clinton's defeat of Bush in the 1992 election pushed Starr back into private practice.

He did not stay out of politics long, however. In 1994, a panel chose Starr to replace Robert Fiske as the independent counsel, the person assigned to pursue charges of wrongdoing against high federal government officials. While no one questioned his honesty or ability, Starr's close ties to conservatives raised questions about whether he was suited to the job. As independent counsel, he was likely to find himself involved in delicate and explosive political situations. A man with Starr's strong Republican leanings who took strong actions against Democrats would lay himself wide open to charges that he was biased. This concern led the *New York Times* to call for his resignation almost as soon as he started his new job.

With momentum again gathering in favor of impeachment, the Republicans' rush to speed the process suddenly began to look suspicious to the Democrats. When the new Congress opened in January, there would be five more Democrats and five fewer Republicans than in the present House. In a close vote on impeachment, a switch of five votes could easily decide the outcome. Therefore, the Republicans had a better chance of impeaching Clinton if the vote took place before the new Congress was sworn in. Democrats complained that allowing the present Congress to vote on impeachment was an attempt to disregard the wishes of the voters.

Starr's original assignment was to investigate possible wrongdoing in the complex financial dealings surrounding the real estate investment venture known as Whitewater. Starr successfully prosecuted three friends of the Clintons on charges of fraud: James McDougal, Arkansas governor Jim Guy Tucker, and Webster Hubbell, who worked at the Rose law firm, where Hillary Clinton was a partner.

McDougal and another man involved in the Whitewater deal hinted that Bill Clinton had been involved in this venture while he was governor of Arkansas. Starr went after McDougal's former wife, Susan, in an effort to get her to testify against Clinton. She refused to cooperate, claiming that Starr and his assistants "wanted me to lie and give them something that was not the truth."

Starr never found evidence that implicated the Clintons in Whitewater and eventually shifted his focus to the Lewinsky–Paula Jones matter. Starr received scorn for spending $40 million investigating Clinton and coming up with nothing but unnecessarily vivid details of an embarrassing private affair. Following President Clinton's acquittal in the Senate, Starr suffered two more defeats when juries failed to convict either Susan McDougal or Judy Hyatt Steele of the obstruction-of-justice charges that Starr had brought. In both cases, Starr's heavy-handed tactics were a major feature of the defense.

When asked to reflect on his handling of the Clinton investigations, Starr observed that Congress had made a major public relations mistake that destroyed the impeachment effort. If he had it to do over again, Starr said, "I would be much more emphatic with the House of Representatives in saying, 'Treat the material cautiously in light of the nature of this material.'"

By this time, the battle lines between Republicans in favor of impeachment and Democrats opposing it had become so plainly drawn that reasoned arguments were not likely to sway most members of either side. With the Republicans controlling a majority of the House, it became increasingly obvious that a vote on impeaching Bill Clinton would come down to a shrinking group of moderate Republicans from the Northeast. As the arguments for and against impeachment grew louder and more shrill, these legislators strained to separate truth from opinion, reason from passion.

Chapter 4

The House Struggles with Impeachment

"WE ARE WORKING for the most courageous people I've ever met, who are determined to do their duty,"[27] said David Schippers, chief counsel for the House Republicans, speaking of the Republican lawmakers who pressed the case for impeachment despite the overwhelming opposition of the public. To critics who charged that the polls proved that Clinton had not lost the confidence of the nation and should therefore not be impeached, the Republicans pointed back to the trial of Andrew Johnson. If the senators in that case had yielded to public opinion, Johnson would have been convicted and ousted as president. Instead, a number of them had defied the mood of the nation and had voted their convictions. Although they had paid a heavy political price, they earned the respect of historians throughout the ages.

As the furious impeachment debate thundered into its

David Schippers, chief counsel for the House Republicans, expressed his admiration for his fellow party members and their handling of the impeachment process.

final stages in early December, Republicans insisted that they were going to do the same thing. "The truth is not decided by the number of scholars with differing opinions, the outcome of polls or by the shifting words of legal opinions," [28] said Schippers. The president had committed grave offenses that required his impeachment. The Republicans would uphold the Constitution even if public opinion made them pay for it.

Perjury Is Perjury

Many of the president's supporters and a large majority of the public believed that Clinton had lied under oath. However, they also believed that the deception was not serious because it dealt with a private matter and because the embarrassing nature of the questions made such lies understandable. The heart of the Republican argument was that perjury is a serious, impeachable offense.

"What is on trial here is the truth and the rule of law," insisted Representative James Sensenbrenner of Wisconsin. He dismissed arguments that Clinton's lies were not serious because they were only about an embarrassing sexual affair that anyone would naturally want to keep hushed up and not about public policy. "Our perjury and false statement statutes do not have various levels of perjury," he noted. As far as the law was concerned, Sensenbrenner saw "no difference between lying about bombing a foreign country and not telling the truth about private sex." [29]

Republican James Sensenbrenner of Wisconsin states that embarrassment over sexual matters was no excuse for Clinton's dishonesty.

David Schippers argued, "The principle that every witness in every case must tell the truth, the whole truth, and nothing but the truth is the foundation of the American system of justice." [30] Clinton had sworn to tell the whole truth but had not done so. Furthermore, there was evidence that he may have tried to get Monica Lewinsky and perhaps others to deceive the courts. By allowing his actions to go unpunished, Congress would encourage lying under oath and tampering with witnesses. If witnesses were not required to tell the truth, how could any person be guaranteed justice in the courts?

Republicans pointed out that dozens of Americans were serving time in prison for the very act of perjury. As to claims that perjury was not a serious enough crime to de-serve impeachment, they pointed to the impeachment case of federal judge Walter Nixon. In 1989, the House of Representatives had voted, 417 to 0, that Judge Nixon's false statements to a grand jury about private financial matters were impeachable offenses. The House impeached him and the Senate con-victed him by wide margins. If a judge could be impeached for per-jury, why should a president be ex-cused for the same offense?

As an example of proof that Clinton did lie under oath, the Republicans offered excerpts

Republican Asa Hutchinson of Arkansas disapproved of the president's lawyers' misleading arguments.

from the president's testimony in both the Paula Jones case and before Ken Starr's grand jury. "Listen to the President's decep-tion yourself,"[31] offered Schippers. He described Clinton's twisted attempts to avoid admitting that he had a sexual rela-tionship with Lewinsky as an insult to the nation's intelligence. In the most ridiculed example, the president at one point asked his questioners to define what they meant by the word "is."

Representative Asa Hutchinson of Arkansas urged the presi-dent's lawyers to simply tell the truth. "Don't play word games,"[32] Hutchinson pleaded.

Republicans argued that, even if one did not want to nitpick about whether Clinton's perjury was a "high crime or misdemeanor," Clinton's behavior was bad enough to deserve impeachment. Through his actions, he had brought ridicule and disgust to the highest office in the land.

Not Impeachable Offenses

The president summoned a host of legal and constitutional experts to argue against impeachment. Their primary argument was that whatever wrongs Clinton had committed, they did not come close to the "high crimes and misdemeanors" standard of the Constitution. "One basic allegation—the president was engaged in an improper relationship which he did not want disclosed—is the core charge that Mr. Starr suggests triggers this grave constitutional crisis," [33] said Abbe Lowell, chief counsel for the House Democrats.

Presidential historian Rob Dalleck agreed that the present charges were trivial compared with the issues surrounding previous impeachment attempts. "President Johnson was impeached after 620,000 Americans were slaughtered, in a bitter contest

Chief counsel Abbe Lowell (pictured) argued that Clinton's alleged relationship with Monica Lewinsky did not come close to the "high crimes and misdemeanor" standard of the Constitution.

over reconstruction. Nixon tried to steal an election. . . . These things are just more substantial." [34]

Yale University professor Bruce Ackerman argued that if, in the past, Congress had used the same low standard for what was an impeachable offense, "our history over the last two centuries would be littered with bills of impeachment." [35] Samuel Beer, a political science expert, testified that Clinton's offenses "don't begin to outweigh the enormous damage of removing a president from office." [36]

Veteran political analyst David Gergen noted that the penalty of impeachment far outweighed the seriousness of the offenses. "A perjurer in a criminal trial never gets the death penalty," [37] he said.

Clinton supporters argued that Republicans were singling out Clinton for especially harsh prosecution far beyond what any ordinary American would experience. According to criminal defense lawyer E. Lawrence Barcella, "No prosecutor except for an independent counsel with unlimited resources would bother trying to build a perjury case where the underlying activity was an adulterous affair." [38] Former U.S. Attorney Thomas Sullivan supported this claim, saying, "The case is so doubtful and weak that a responsible prosecutor would not present it to a grand jury." [39]

Former U.S. attorney general Nicholas Katzenbach argued that the nation's founders intended impeachment as a last resort to remove a president whose actions were so severe that the nation could no longer trust him to perform his duties. "The fundamental question," said Katzenbach, "is whether the President had done something which has destroyed public confidence in his ability to continue in that office." Noting Clinton's high standing in public opinion polls, he asked, "If the public doesn't believe that what he has done seriously affects his ability to perform his public duties as president, should the committee conclude that his acts have destroyed public confidence?" [40]

Clinton supporters tried gentle pleading to get the Republicans to back away from impeachment. The president's lawyers sympathized with those who were upset with the president's conduct and testimony. "The President was evasive, incomplete, misleading, even maddening,"[41] admitted White House attorneys. But that did not change the fact that Clinton's offenses were not what the founding fathers had had in mind when they laid out a process for impeachment. As far as needing to punish the president, Clinton's public humiliation was already a far more severe punishment than any ordinary American would have had to endure for similar actions.

"Orange Hair and Floppy Shoes"

Democrats and some moderate Republicans continued their efforts to resolve the issue by substituting a strongly worded resolution condemning Clinton's actions. In mid-December, Clinton tried to support their attempt. He delivered a speech in the rose garden of the White House in which he apologized for his actions and agreed to accept such a resolution from Congress.

Clinton, in a statement made from the rose garden of the White House, apologized for his actions and agreed to accept a resolution from Congress.

But it was too little, too late. Noting that Clinton still refused to admit that he had lied under oath, the Republican majority on the House Judiciary Committee refused to allow the House to vote on a resolution of censure. From this point, there could be no compromise, no avoiding a vote on impeachment. The goal of a bipartisan search for the truth degenerated into heated name-calling and accusations. Democrats stepped up their attacks on Starr. Sean Willentz, professor of history at Princeton University, warned the Republicans that they risked "going down in history with the zealots and the fanatics."[42]

Such words only inflamed Republicans, who resented having their motives questioned. The House Judiciary Committee began voting on articles of impeachment even before Clinton's defense witnesses finished testifying.

The bitter squabbling between the parties saddened and disgusted the majority of Americans. John Dean, a lawyer who had been caught in the middle of the Watergate scandal while working for the Nixon administration, expressed a common feeling when he said, "I'm embarrassed." According to Dean, the political fighting in Washington "makes the infamous partisan impeachment of Andrew Johnson in 1868 look good."[43]

Not only did the two parties fight over the issues, they also fought over who was responsible for the bad feelings between parties. Democrats accused the Republicans of turning the whole impeachment issue into a one-sided ambush of the president. Republican campaign adviser Ed Gillespie shot back that the Democrats were the ones putting politics above justice. "They showed up with orange hair and floppy shoes and complained about what a circus this has become,"[44] said Gillespie.

The Articles of Impeachment

The House Judiciary Committee voted on four articles of impeachment. The Republicans held a twenty-one to sixteen edge in committee members, and all the articles passed on strict party lines—Republicans voted in favor, Democrats against.

Article 1 focused on Clinton's testimony before the grand jury on August 17, 1998. The basic charge was that the president

AN EXPLOSIVE COMMITTEE

Although legislators from both parties realized that a bipartisan effort would be needed to resolve the impeachment issues, that effort was doomed from the start. According to House rules, the impeachment inquiry would have to start in the Judiciary Committee. Of all the committees in Congress, the House Judiciary Committee was the most divided, outspoken, and politically explosive.

On the Republican side, Bob Barr of Georgia had tried to get Clinton impeached for dishonesty long before the Lewinsky scandal. On the Democrat side, Maxine Waters of California had publicly accused the CIA of dealing crack in Los Angeles.

Relations between Republicans and Democrats were so frayed that, at one tense meeting shortly before his death, Republican congressman Sonny Bono had tried to lighten the mood by ordering out for pizza. The gesture did not work. Republicans retired to one room to eat their pizza while the Democrats went to another.

According to political experts, the hostile atmosphere of the Judiciary Committee was no accident. This committee was assigned to deal with many of the most controversial issues, such as abortion, gun control, and affirmative action. These are the issues on which Democrats and Republicans disagree the most and which are the most important to their active party members back home. As a result, neither side believes they can afford to lose any battles in this committee. According to *Newsweek*, "When party leaders make assignments, they want true believers." They stock the committee with their toughest and most passionate members. Republicans on the committee tend to be much more conservative than most Republicans while Democrats tend to be much more liberal than most Democrats.

Although this strategy protects the parties on some of their most cherished core issues, it causes headaches for anyone trying to find the common ground necessary to deal with an issue like impeachment.

had committed perjury. The article accused him of having "willfully corrupted and manipulated the judicial process of the United States for his personal gain." It charged that he "willfully provided perjurious, false, and misleading testimony to the grand jury"[45] about his relationship with Monica Lewinsky and had allowed his attorney to make false statements as well.

Article 2 dealt with Clinton's testimony in the Paula Jones case. Again, it accused Clinton of lying about his relationship

*Chairman of the Judiciary Committee Henry Hyde (far right) presents the
Articles of Impeachment to the Secretary of the Senate Gary Sisco (far left).*

with Lewinsky. This was the only article on which one of the
Republicans, Lindsay Graham, voted with the Democrats. Graham noted that, legally, in order for a lie to be perjury, it had to
be relevant to the case. The judge had ruled that Clinton's testimony on the Lewinsky matter was not important to the Jones
case. Therefore, said Graham, it was not perjury. But his Republican colleagues disagreed.

Article 3 accused Clinton of a pattern of obstructing justice.
This included urging Lewinsky to lie in a civil suit, having
friends find a high-paying job for Lewinsky to ensure her silence,
concealing evidence of his relationship with Lewinsky by asking
her to secretly return gifts he had given her, giving false statements to potential witnesses to mislead them into reporting
falsely, and not correcting statements made by his attorney that
Clinton knew to be false.

Article 4 charged that the president "willfully made false and
misleading public statements for the purpose of deceiving the
American people, misled aides, and used executive privilege frivo-

lously."[46] This last charge had to do with Clinton's view that aides and Secret Service individuals did not have to cooperate with Starr's investigation because the interests of the nation required the president to be able to trust those around him to keep secrets.

The impeachment charges summed up by saying, "In all of the above, William Jefferson Clinton has undermined the integrity of his office, has brought disrepute on the Presidency, and has betrayed his trust as President."[47]

Wagging the Dog?

The House vote on the impeachment charges was scheduled for December 16. Just before it was to take place, however, the Clinton administration announced the beginning of air strikes against Iraq. According to Defense Department officials, the military measures were necessary because Iraq had repeatedly violated its agreements

Just before the House was supposed to vote on the impeachment charges, Clinton ordered a series of air strikes against Iraq. This led to speculation that the administration was trying to direct attention away from the trial.

to allow international inspectors to monitor the country for nuclear, chemical, and biological weapons development. The latest deadline for Iraq to comply with the agreements was now up.

Immediately, a cloud of suspicion arose in Congress. The timing seemed strangely similar to the plot of a recent popular movie called *Wag the Dog*, in which a United States president concocted a phony war to deflect press attention from a scandal. Republican senator Trent Lott of Mississippi said, "Both the timing and the policy are open to question."[48]

Democrats responded angrily that Republicans were trying to make a political issue out of an important military concern when they ought to be backing American troops who were risking their lives in missions over Iraq. They pointed out that Clinton's secretary of defense, the man in charge of overseeing military operations, was William Cohen, a Republican, who would not have approved the air strikes simply to help Clinton.

Republican congressman Richard Armey shot back that "the suspicions some people have about the president's motives in this attack is itself a powerful argument for impeachment."[49]

After a quick and furious debate, the House agreed to postpone voting on the impeachment articles for one day only.

Livingston's Bombshell

There was more drama awaiting the House of Representatives on the following day. Republican House leader Livingston had come under fire in recent days because of devastating new information about his personal life. When publisher Larry Flynt had bought a full-page ad in the *Washington Post* in October offering $1 million for information about sexual misdeeds of Republican legislators, several people came forward with charges that Livingston had been involved in sexual affairs of his own. Since one of the impeachment articles claimed that Clinton had disgraced the office of the presidency because of his conduct, Democrats cited this as an example of hypocrisy.

When Livingston rose before the House and solemnly asked the president to resign to save the country from the turmoil of an impeachment trial, several irate Democrats aware of Livingston's past called out that Livingston should resign himself. To their astonishment, that is exactly what Livingston did. In explaining his decision to step down, Livingston said, "I must

---

HENRY HYDE: CAUGHT IN THE CROSSFIRE

Before the Starr report arrived at the House of Representatives, Henry Hyde enjoyed a reputation as one of the most respected people in Congress. Conservatives viewed him as an articulate champion of the antiabortion movement. Liberals considered him a fair man. Barney Frank, one of the most liberal Democrats in the House, praised Hyde as "a man of dignity; he knows the rules, and he follows the rules."

Hyde grew up in a working-class section of Chicago in a family of loyal Democrats. He attended Georgetown University on a basketball scholarship and then spent two years in the navy during World War II. His war experiences and his studies made him suspicious of Communists. Believing that the Democrats did not take a tough enough stance against communism, he switched to the Republican Party in the 1950s. It was not until 1975 that he won a seat in Congress. Upholding his reputation for fair-mindedness, he supported Bill Clinton on issues such as gun control and voting rights.

Hyde was the man most responsible for guiding the impeachment inquiry in the House of Representatives. As the split between Democrats and Republicans widened on the issue, the task of keeping order became incredibly difficult. The worse the bickering, the more Hyde's reputation for fairness suffered. Critics called Hyde a hypocrite for probing Clinton's sex life when he himself had once had an affair with a married woman. And Hyde's own words came back to haunt him. In supporting President Reagan's deception in secretly selling arms to Iran in the 1980s, Hyde had said, "It just seems too simplistic to condemn all lying." Now that Clinton was caught in a lie, said Hyde's critics, he suddenly seemed to think lying was an impeachable offense.

The steady barrage of criticism seemed to harden Hyde's stance. By the time the Senate trial began, he had come to view the impeachment as a matter of honor. He wondered out loud if a United States with Clinton acquitted was worth saving.

Hyde's fervor in prosecuting the president cost him. He was unable to convince the public that he was handling the matter fairly. Before the impeachment inquiry, *Newsweek* predicted, "If the crisis comes and he can't keep order, the public may be so disgusted that it'll decide even a sinful president looks good by comparison."

That is exactly what happened.

Republican House leader Robert Livingston surprised Democrats by resigning his position following the charge that he had had past sexual affairs.

set an example that I hope President Clinton will follow." [50]

Even Democrats were dismayed at the depths to which the impeachment battle had sunk. Some of them begged Livingston to reconsider. Richard Gephardt of Missouri pleaded with lawmakers from both parties to stop the politics of slash and burn that was destroying the lives of capable politicians.

Clinton, however, was unmoved. Claiming that resignation would be a surrender to those who wished to overturn the results of the American voters, he declared he had no intention of resigning. Dismayed by the failure of Livingston's bold move to end the conflict, Representative Bob Franks of New Jersey said, "The president continues to put his own self-interest ahead of the interests of the nation." [51]

But others suggested that the partisan impeachment effort had made resignation impossible. "A case for resignation existed months ago, when the scandal broke," said David Gergen. "But his stepping down now would seriously damage the highest office in the land." [52] It would now appear as though the president was hounded from office by his enemies.

Poisoned Atmosphere

Meanwhile, the moderate Republicans who had resisted impeachment came under increasing pressure from both sides. The Republican leadership made a secret, last-ditch effort to win the votes of
the undecided congresspersons. They brought their colleagues into
a locked room and showed them evidence that Starr had gathered
but had not included in his impeachment report. The evidence was
testimony from a woman identified only as Jane Doe Five, who
claimed that Clinton had forced her into unwanted sex twenty years
earlier. No proof was offered to support her claims, and Starr had not
considered the information reliable enough to include in his report.
Nonetheless, the woman's story was upsetting and raised the possibility that the nation's highest office was held by an unreformed
sexual offender.

One by one, previously undecided Republicans announced
their intention to vote against the president on at least some of
the articles of impeachment. Jack Quinn of New York had previously opposed impeachment. Now he said that "the more I
learn about the serious details of perjury and obstruction of justice, the more I am concerned about the President's failure to
tell the truth under oath."[53]

The Impeachment Vote

On December 19, 1998, the House of Representatives met to finally decide the issue. Thomas M. Davis III of Virginia spoke for
many congresspersons when he said that he hated to get out of
bed that day. The result that seemed almost impossible just a
month or so earlier now seemed inevitable. The vote would be
close, but lawmakers on both sides now expected Clinton to be
impeached. Whatever happened, it would be a sad day for the
United States. Through his actions, President Clinton had
brought shame to the nation. With its bitter and vicious squabbling certain to end in a power struggle between the two sides,
Congress would only add to that shame.

After weeks of agonizing debate, Sherwood Boehlert had finally made up his mind. The president, he decided, had been
"blinded by his contempt for people he thought were out to get

AMERICANS JUDGE THE CASE

Most political experts conceded that impeachment was virtually impossible without widespread public support. Public opinion was strongly against Andrew Johnson when he came within a razor's edge of being impeached. Richard Nixon's job approval rating had sunk to around 24 percent when the House began drafting impeachment articles against him.

In the case of Bill Clinton, however, public support for impeachment never appeared. A strong majority of the nation did not believe that the Starr investigation had produced the "substantial and credible evidence of impeachable offenses" that it claimed.

That is not to say that Americans approved of Clinton's actions. There were a few times when a majority of voters thought he should resign for the good of the country. The public gave him extremely low ratings for morality, trustworthiness, and honesty. Nearly four out of five Americans believed that the president testified falsely before a grand jury.

But roughly two out of three Americans opposed his impeachment. That number believed that Clinton was performing well in his duties as president, that the Lewinsky matter was a private affair that should not have been under investigation, that the release of the taped grand jury testimony was inappropriate, and that the Senate should end the impeachment trial as quickly as possible.

him"[54] and had violated the law. Therefore, Boehlert would vote in favor of Articles 1 and 2 charging Clinton with perjury in his grand jury testimony and Paula Jones testimony. But he did not think the evidence supported Articles 3 and 4 dealing with obstruction of justice.

The Democrats made a futile last gesture to stave off impeachment by asking for a vote on the resolution of censure. They held out hope that if moderate Republicans were allowed to vote for this, they would not feel the need to vote for impeachment. But again, the Republican leadership did not allow the vote. Furious, the Democrats walked out of the House together in protest.

When they returned, voting began on House Resolution 611, the impeachment of Bill Clinton. Most observers considered the first article, which accused Clinton of lying under oath, as having the strongest support. If it did not pass, neither would any of the others, and Clinton would escape the threat of impeachment once and for all. If it did pass, he would be the first elected president ever impeached.

As the votes were counted, it was obvious that the vote would be along strict party lines, just as the Judiciary Committee vote had been. Out of 434 representatives, only five Democrats voted in favor of the article, and only five Republicans voted against it. At 1:22 P.M. the vote was official. By a slim margin of 228 to 206, Clinton was impeached.

Article 2, concerning perjury in the Paula Jones case, failed by a vote of 229 to 205. The closest voting of all came on Article 3, the obstruction-of-justice charge. The House approved that article, 221 to 212. It then solidly rejected the abuse-of-power charges in Article 4 by 285 to 148.

At last, the impeachment battle that had consumed the energy of the House for four months was over. But the damage had been done. "The House that voted to impeach President Clinton is more deeply divided than at any time since the Reconstruction,"[55] said *U.S. News & World Report*. The hard feelings that had erupted during the impeachment process threatened to block any attempts to work together for the nation's interest.

Chapter 5

The Senate Trial

A FTER VIEWING THE mud-slinging, name-calling spectacle of the House impeachment process, the senators dreaded the task that had been handed to them. They were acutely aware that the American people were disgusted by the partisan way the House had handled the matter. A strong majority of the public wanted Congress to drop the impeachment charges and get on with the business of governing.

A Trial That Neither Side Wants

Both the Republicans and Democrats desperately searched for a way to avoid a long, bitter Senate trial. They knew that Clinton was determined to fight for his presidency with every legal weapon at his disposal. One of the president's lawyers said that if they were forced to defend Clinton on every point of law and fact raised, their defense could take a year and a half. For the Senate to be tied up in this scandal for that amount of time would paralyze the government, creating a national disaster that would make the House squabble look like a trivial disagreement.

Republican senators were also concerned with the beating their party's image had taken during the House deliberations. By and large, the public blamed them for the ugly bipartisan battle, particularly because they refused to even allow a vote on a resolution of censure. According to polls, a majority of Americans viewed the impeachment effort as little more than a Republican effort to destroy a president whom they disliked personally. They wanted it stopped. The longer the impeachment process dragged on, the more the Republicans would suffer for it.

The Democrats' leader in the Senate, Tom Daschle of South Dakota, could not understand why the Republicans would continue to commit political suicide. "Talk about being off message," he said. "Republicans are so consumed by this they still don't get it. It's a wonderful situation for us." [56]

Although the impeachment mess was helping the Democrats by raising public distrust of the Republicans, President Clinton had his own reasons for wanting it ended as quickly as possible. The details of the affair with Lewinsky were humiliating. The last thing he wanted was for this scandal to stay in the public spotlight all through the one-and-a-half-year defense that his lawyers threatened.

Also, Clinton could no longer be certain that the Senate would acquit him of the impeachment charges. On the surface, he appeared to have no worries. Unlike the House, where a simple majority could impeach him, the Senate required a two-thirds majority. That meant sixty-seven votes were needed to convict. The Republicans controlled only fifty-five seats in the Senate, while the Democrats had forty-five. If his support among Democrats remained intact, his presidency was safe.

On the other hand, Clinton had never expected the House to impeach him. The Senate, in general, was even more unpredictable than the House. Senators on both sides insisted they had no idea how they might vote on the issue. Statements like that of New York Democrat Daniel Moynihan both confused and worried Clinton supporters. Moynihan said that the Republicans were right in saying that perjury was an impeachable offense. "It does not follow that the Senate will vote for impeachment, however," [57] he added. Did that mean he would vote for or against impeachment? Leon Panetta, who had once served as a top aide to Clinton, noted that any legal case "is risky enough when you take it to a jury, and here you are dealing with 100 political egos." [58]

Looking for a Way Out

On January 5, 1999, two weeks after the House impeachment vote, four Republican and four Democratic senators met privately with

Senators were often unpredictable when it came to deciding on the impeachment issue. New York Democrat Daniel Moynihan answered questions concerning the trial with vague responses.

Senate majority leader Trent Lott. Strom Thurmond, the ninety-six-year-old Republican senator from South Carolina, put the matter simply: "It takes a two-thirds vote to get rid of this fellow. We don't have it. Let's get it over." [59]

The leaders of the two parties in the Senate, Lott and Daschle, met frequently in an attempt to work out a plan that would avoid partisan bickering. At one point they suggested a proposal by Republican Slade Gorton of Washington and Democrat Joseph Lieberman that would allow one day for the prosecution to outline the charges and then one day for the president's lawyers to respond. At that point, the Senate would take a preliminary vote on whether the charges against Clinton were actually the high crimes and misdemeanors cited by the Constitution. If the Senate decided they were not, they could avoid a trial of whether Clinton actually committed such offenses.

The House Republicans were enraged by such talk. They had appointed a team of thirteen congressmen, all Republicans, to prosecute the case in the Senate. These thirteen, known as the "House managers," believed strongly that the president's misdeeds were so great that he must be removed from office, and they were determined to do everything in their power to win a conviction from the Senate. They considered any attempts to sweep the impeachment charges under the rug as a slap in the face to the Republican congresspersons who had laid their political careers on the line to vote for impeachment. Even more important, they argued, the Constitution required a Senate trial on any impeachment charges brought by the House. Conservative Republican voters were also outraged at the idea that their own party leaders were helping Clinton wriggle off the hook so easily.

Senate majority leader Trent Lott and Senate minority leader Tom Daschle were unable to eliminate partisan quarreling.

Faced with this opposition, Republican senators backed away from plans to short-circuit the trial. But they continued to look for ways to take care of the matter quickly and in an atmosphere of respect.

TRENT LOTT: THE MAN IN THE MIDDLE

"I think you can accomplish an awful lot if you're open and try to do what's right on a personal basis and also what's right for the country," said Senator Trent Lott. "Sometimes that forces you to do things you don't philosophically agree with." The impeachment process would put Lott's optimistic theory to the test.

The fifty-five-year-old Lott grew up in the gulf coast of Mississippi. His mother was a teacher and his father was a shipyard worker with a drinking problem. In school, Lott developed the ability to work or play with any group of kids, no matter how different. That ability, as well as his southern charm and booming bass voice, served him well in his chosen career as a lawyer and a politician.

Lott began his political career as an aide to a Democratic congressman from Mississippi in 1968. But his views became increasingly conservative over the years. When the congressman retired in 1972, Lott ran for the seat as a Republican. He rose rapidly in the ranks. After only a few years on the job, he won the post of Republican whip, the person in charge of lining up votes on key issues for his or her party.

After sixteen years in the House, he ran for and won a Senate seat in 1988. His leadership qualities were just as apparent in the Senate as they had been in the House. When the Republicans gained control of the Senate, Lott took over as the Senate majority leader. That position put him at center stage when the House voted to impeach Clinton. As majority leader, it was his job to direct the course of the trial.

For Lott, it was a ticklish position. Conservatives expected him to go after Clinton aggressively and work for impeachment. On the other hand, other Republicans were concerned about the battering that Republicans were taking in the polls because of their impeachment stand. As one of them said, "Trent's not going to force us to walk a political plank if it's unnecessary."

Furthermore, Lott was known as a controlling person who could not stand to have even a hair out of place. The idea of his Senate degenerating into the kind of political food fight that he had seen in the House alarmed him. He worked closely with the Democrats' Senate leader, Tom Daschle of South Dakota, to keep the proceedings as smooth and spite-free as possible.

Witnesses or No Witnesses?

In negotiations between Republicans and Democrats concerning the ground rules for the trial, the main sticking point was the matter of witnesses. Democrats did not want them. They noted that once you started bringing in witnesses, there would be no way of avoiding the long, bitter trial that few of the senators wanted. Senator Daschle noted that Ken Starr had already submitted sixty thousand pages of evidence on the impeachment issues. Included in that was the grand jury testimony of everyone who had the slightest link to the case. What was the point of bringing in witnesses to rehash their sworn testimony? In addition, the House of Representatives had not seen the need to call witnesses before voting to impeach the president. Daschle and others asked why the very same people who had voted on impeachment without hearing from witnesses now insisted that witnesses were necessary in order for senators to judge the case.

Both Republican and Democratic senators worried about the nature of some of the testimony of the witnesses. A large part of the perjury case against the president had to do with his relationship with Lewinsky. The senators did not want the kind of sordid details included in the Starr report to muddy the dignity of the Senate.

The House managers, however, noted that prosecutors in any trial had the right to bring in any witnesses they thought were necessary to presenting their case. They insisted that they be given the same courtesy and that they be given the freedom to present their case fully. Senator James Inhofe criticized his colleagues' efforts to block witnesses. "That's a whitewash and a shirking of our responsibility that the Constitution gave us," he declared. "How can someone vote without hearing from witnesses and without hearing all the evidence?"[60]

Postponing the Key Decision

The arguments over allowing witnesses threatened to bring about the same bipartisan fighting that had marred the House's impeachment hearings. That matter was still unresolved when Chief Justice William Rehnquist opened the trial on January 7.

Senators swear in at Clinton's impeachment hearing. The senators had to swear that they would be impartial and fair before the impeachment hearing could commence.

The first order of business was for all senators to swear they would judge the case fairly and impartially. Then Henry Hyde, at the head of the thirteen House managers, presented the two articles of impeachment against Clinton.

The next order of business was to adopt the rules of the trial. Republicans and Democrats each had their own versions of these rules, the main difference being whether or not to allow witnesses. The Republicans could have adopted their own rules by a simple majority vote, but they desperately wanted to avoid actions that would make it appear as if they were unfairly trying to get the president. Before adopting the rules, the Senate met as an informal group known as a caucus to decide their goals and strategy. Normally, a caucus is a meeting of members of only one political party. This evening's caucus, however, was a joint meeting of both parties.

Lott and Daschle worked hard to find a compromise that both parties could accept. At the end of a three-hour meeting, they got the Senate to approve the rules of the trial by a 100 to 0 vote, on the condition that they postpone a decision about witnesses until later in the trial.

University of Michigan law professor Yale Kamisar noted that this was a strange way to start a trial. "In no other kind of proceeding do you have this kind of piecemeal approach where you get started and see how things develop and then decide what to do," [61] said Kamisar. But the Senate was in a unique position. Impeachments were so rare and the Constitution so sketchy on the matter that the Senate could make up the rules any way it wished.

What Standard of Proof?

Tradition is important to the U.S. Senate, so the senators based many of their decisions about how to proceed on the Andrew Johnson trial. One of the main issues was a definition of the role of the senators. In a normal trial, a panel of jurors decides whether the defendant is guilty or not guilty. Jurors are expected to consider only the evidence. Any juror with even a hint of prejudice is quickly dismissed from the jury.

But in the Clinton case, as with Johnson's, there were senators with clear conflicts of interest. Three of them were newly elected senators who had been in the House of Representatives and had already voted on the impeachment there. Senator Barbara Boxer of California was related to Clinton by marriage. Senator Tim Hutchinson of Arkansas was the brother of one of the House managers prosecuting the case.

Furthermore, in criminal cases, a judge tightly controls the trial. He or she instructs a jury in the interpretation of the law, decides what evidence to allow, and determines what behavior is permissible in the courtroom. Based on the Johnson trial, the Senate did not give this control to Chief Justice Rehnquist. Although he could make rulings, any of his decisions could be overridden by a majority vote. In effect, he would serve more as a master of ceremonies than as a judge.

These situations underscored the point that an impeachment trial is a unique situation, different from any criminal trial.

Chief Justice Rehnquist (above, being sworn in) was not given complete control of the impeachment trial. The majority was at liberty to override any of his decisions.

Former federal judge Alcee Hastings found that out when he had tried to bring in criminal standards in his own impeachment trial. He argued that, in judging his case, the senators should use the same burden of proof required in criminal cases: that the accused is innocent unless proven guilty beyond a reasonable doubt. The Senate rejected his argument. But while debating the issue, the senators could come to no agreement on what standard of proof they should use.

The result was that the senators would serve as a unique combination of judge and jury. Each was free to decide the case as he or she wished, using whatever reasoning or criteria seemed best. They were under no obligation to follow any rule except their own conscience, and they did not have to explain their vote to anyone. Their decision was final. Unlike criminal cases, the defendant could not appeal the decision to another court. This was, in fact, what the framers of the Constitution had intended, for impeachment is not a criminal trial but a political one. Those who sat in judgment were expected to consider not only the facts of the case but also what was best for the entire country.

The Rules

Although the senators were entirely on their own in making their decisions, many of the procedures of the trial were strictly controlled. The senators agreed to continue the trial uninterrupted from Monday through Saturday each week until its conclusion. In order to allow Rehnquist to carry out his duties on the Supreme Court, however, the trial would be scheduled only for the afternoons.

Only the House managers, the president's defense team, and the president of the Senate would be allowed to speak during the trial. If senators had any comments while the impeachment trial was in session, they would have to put them in writing to the judge. As in the Johnson impeachment trial, the trial would be open to the public at all times, except for when the Senate met to discuss the case prior to voting. At that time, the doors of the Senate would be closed and all discussions kept private.

The House Managers Open

The House managers were frustrated that the issue of allowing witnesses had been postponed. They felt that witnesses were so important to their case that they spent much of their opening arguments trying to persuade the senators to allow them. This used up valuable time that they had intended to spend presenting their facts.

The senators, who were accustomed to free debate on issues, sat in eerie silence as five representatives spent six hours laying out the evidence against the president.

James Sensenbrenner of Wisconsin opened the House managers' argument by saying, "No man is above the law and no man is below it." The president, in lying before a grand jury and using his influence to prevent the truth from coming out, "decided to put himself above the law not once, not twice, but repeatedly." To those who claimed that telling a lie did not amount to a high crime or misdemeanor, Sensenbrenner declared that "perjury is the twin brother of bribery."[62] Bribery is one act specifically cited in the Constitution as being an impeachable offense.

 ## WILLIAM REHNQUIST: NO-NONSENSE JUDGE

The solicitor general stood before the nine Supreme Court justices, pleading his case. "I would like to offer to share with you a bit of the record," he started.

Chief Justice Rehnquist looked down at him sternly. "Why don't you just tell us?"

The solicitor general who felt the sting of Rehnquist's legendary disdain for flowery and self-important speech was Kenneth Starr. More than a decade after that incident, Rehnquist would hold the gavel as the Senate met to judge the impeachment articles that Starr had helped forge.

The seventy-four-year-old Rehnquist was a product of the suburbs of Milwaukee. A brilliant student, he had graduated first in his Stanford law class of 1952. He had worked as a lawyer in Phoenix until President Nixon noticed his activity on behalf of the Republican Party. Nixon brought him to Washington to serve as assistant attorney general and then nominated him to a position on the Supreme Court in 1971. Upon the retirement of Warren Burger in 1986, President Reagan named him chief justice.

Rehnquist quickly won marks for his skill in managing the Supreme Court. Unlike Burger, who was disorganized and often let sessions ramble on for hours, Rehnquist held a tight rein on all proceedings. He had no patience with those who tried to bend the rules, and he frequently stopped lawyers in midsentence when their time was up. Although he was a conservative Republican, even the most liberal members of the court praised him for his fairness.

Rehnquist came to the impeachment trial with suspicions about the impeachment process. In a book called *Grand Inquests*, he wrote that impeachment could easily become a partisan exercise. Rehnquist also disdained the limelight that many of the senators seemed to enjoy. He had worked hard to keep a low profile as chief justice and he did not like being in front of the cameras at the trial. During the trial, he stayed out of the way as much as possible, allowing the Senate to proceed according to its rules. But the senators found out that even they were not immune to the embarrassing slap of Rehnquist's impatience. During the secret discussions prior to the vote, each senator was given fifteen minutes to speak. Several were in midsentence when the gavel came down, telling them to sit down because their time was up.

James Rogan of California stepped in to plead for a chance to present all the evidence. After citing contradictory statements from many grand jury witnesses in the case, he said, "So who is telling the truth? The only way to really know is to bring forth witnesses, put them under oath, and give each juror, each member of this body, the opportunity to make that determination of credibility." [63]

Representative Ed Bryant of Tennessee responded to those who had criticized the House for voting to impeach without hearing from witnesses and now demanding that the Senate hear them. He pointed out that the Constitution did not intend for Congress to conduct two separate trials. The House was given the duty of bringing a president's misconduct to light by impeaching him. The Senate—and only the Senate—had the responsibility of conducting a thorough trial.

Hutchinson and Obstruction of Justice

Obstruction-of-justice laws are among the most broad and vaguely defined laws on the books. According to Professor Pamela Bucy of the University of Alabama Law School, "You've got to have broadly drawn statutes because people who engage in obstruction of justice are generally very creative, very clever at achieving their ends." [64] But that also means that there is often a very fuzzy line between being uncooperative or unhelpful and trying to block the truth from coming out.

Asa Hutchinson of Arkansas, a former prosecutor, did a masterful job of drawing that line in the case against Clinton. He detailed seven acts by which Clinton actively tried to prevent the truth from coming out. According to Hutchinson, the obstruction began on December 5, 1997, when Monica Lewinsky's name first appeared on a list of potential witnesses who might be called to testify in the Paula Jones case. Hutchinson contended that Clinton discussed possible cover stories with Lewinsky to conceal the nature of their relationship. When Lewinsky was called on for her testimony in the case, Clinton encouraged her to file a false affidavit and tried to hide the fact that he had given her gifts. He then got his friend Vernon Jordan to find a good job for Lewinsky to buy her cooperation.

Asa Hutchinson of Arkansas argued that Clinton attempted to cover up his affair with Lewinsky, in violation of the obstruction-of-justice laws.

In the Paula Jones case, Hutchinson argued, Clinton had sat silently while his lawyer stated that Clinton had never had any type of relationship with Lewinsky. When Starr's investigation closed in on his web of lies, the president tried to corruptly influence the testimony of his secretary, Betty Currie. According to Currie's own testimony, Clinton had asked her to confirm his memory of having never been alone with Lewinsky. At the time, Clinton knew that Currie was a potential witness, claimed Hutchinson, so his conversation could only be described as an attempt to influence her testimony. Finally, Clinton gave false accounts of his relationship with Lewinsky to his aides, knowing that they might be called to testify on the matter.

Hutchinson was especially persuasive in describing the situation surrounding Lewinsky's job search. Using charts and a timeline as visual aids, he showed that the search for a job for Lewinsky began to get serious immediately after the president learned, on December 10, that she was definitely on the witness list for the Jones case.

"At every turn," said Hutchinson, "he used whatever means available to evade the truth, destroy evidence, tamper with witnesses." [65]

Continuing the Attack

More House managers stepped to the front of the Senate the next day to continue the attack. Representative Bill McCollom of Florida bolstered Hutchinson's arguments and countered criticism that the impeachment was based on nothing but a private sexual affair that had nothing to do with the duties and responsibilities of the president. "This is not about sex," said McCollom. "This is about obstruction of justice. This is about a pattern. This is about a scheme. This is about a lot of lies." [66]

Representative Lindsay Graham of South Carolina cited evidence from the impeachment case of federal judge Henry Claiborne to support this position. He quoted former senator Charles Mathias of Maryland, who declared in that case, "Impeachable conduct does not have to occur in the performance of an officer's official duties." [67] Clinton's conduct, said Graham, was serious because he tried to prevent Paula Jones from exercising her legal right to the facts of Clinton's conduct with Lewinsky.

Representative Steve Buyer of Indiana pounded home Sensenbrenner's argument that perjury was a serious offense worthy of impeachment. If lying under oath in court was such a minor crime, Buyer asked, then why were 115 persons presently serving time in federal prisons for committing perjury?

Courtroom Dramatics

The relentless barrage against Clinton was broken up by Senator Tom Harkin's bold maneuver. During his presentation, Representative Bob Barr of Georgia repeatedly referred to the senators as *jurors*. Harkin rose to his feet and objected to the term, breaking the ban on speech that all senators had so far observed. "We are not just triers of fact and law," [68] he insisted. The Senate's duty went beyond determining guilt or innocence; it was a question of whether impeachment was good for the nation. Chief Justice Rehnquist agreed with his objection and asked the prosecution to stop using the term *jurors*.

Representative Henry Hyde finished the House managers' presentation with a flourish of his own. In an impassioned twenty-minute speech, he pleaded with the senators to put aside their personal views and judge the facts. "This case is a test of whether what the founding fathers described as 'sacred honor' still has meaning," he declared. Then he quoted a letter from a third grader who said, "If you cannot believe the President, who can you believe?"[69] Hyde summed up by saying that men had died on the beaches of Normandy in World War II and elsewhere to uphold the Constitution. The Senate should not cheapen the sacrifice made by these people by letting a man who had violated that Constitution remain in office.

The experts conceded that the House managers had made a strong case for conviction. Many Democrats admitted that their arguments were more effective than they had expected. Republicans began to waver on the question of calling witnesses. It seemed Clinton's presidency was in danger again.

Chapter 6

The Senate Decides

IT DID NOT take long for the momentum to switch back in the president's favor. The president's lawyers picked apart the House managers' case point by point. Attorney Charles Ruff landed the most devastating blow against Hutchinson's obstruction-of-justice presentation. Hutchinson's charts had shown that Vernon Jordan, at the president's request, had begun serious efforts to land

Attorney Charles Ruff countered Hutchinson's argument by asserting that Vernon Jordan had attempted to secure a job for Lewinsky before Judge Wright announced her decision.

Lewinsky a job on December 11. That happened to be the same day that Judge Wright announced her decision to allow testimony about the president's relations with other women. Obviously, said Hutchinson, the president's friend moved into high gear to buy Lewinsky's silence as soon as he found out that she would be called as a witness in the Jones trial.

But Ruff displayed evidence that Jordan met with Lewinsky at 1:15 P.M. on December 11. That was a full five or six hours before Judge Wright made her decision known. By the time she did announce the decision, Jordan was already on a plane to Amsterdam. Hutchinson's claim had simply been wrong.

Defense Against Obstruction

Ruff and his associate in the defense, Cheryl Mills, blasted the House managers for recklessly throwing a mishmash of charges around in the hopes that one of them would stick. They noted that the president's secretary, Betty Currie, had already given her testimony before the conversation in which Clinton supposedly coached her on what to say.

Ruff observed that much of the managers' case relied on evidence from the Jones lawsuit. That was illegal because the House had rejected the articles of impeachment that were based on that case. According to the Constitution, only the House of Representatives can bring impeachment charges before the Senate. The managers cannot bring in any charges not approved by the House. Yet the managers, said Ruff, "have treated these articles as empty vessels" [70] that they can fill with any charges they like.

Concerning the claim that Clinton and Lewinsky had taken back presents to hide them from prosecutors, Ruff showed that these presents had been returned before the phone call that the managers had cited as the arrangement for the gifts to be picked up. Ruff noted that, in fact, the president had given Lewinsky more gifts the same day he had picked up the gifts in question. Was that the work of someone conspiring to hide evidence?

Mills argued that the House managers used only one of ten different accounts of events that Lewinsky had given in order to cast suspicion on the president. The managers also ignored the fact that Lewinsky had said under oath that she was not pressured to lie in her affidavit.

On the issue of whether the president committed perjury by hiding behind strained definitions of legal terms, Ruff argued that Clinton was only using legal protections to safeguard the rights of the accused.

White House attorney Gregory Craig explained that the law required four elements to sustain a charge of perjury. There must be an oath, an intent to lie, and a false statement, and the false statement must be important to the case. Craig argued that, according to the president's definition of *sexual relations*, he was not lying when he said that he did not have sexual relations with Lewinsky. Even if others did not accept his definition, Clinton could not be accused of intent to lie. Even more important, the false statements with which he was charged were not of crucial importance to any existing case. Craig brought out videotaped testimony from federal prosecutors who said that proving perjury requires two or more witnesses or a great deal of surrounding evidence. That burden of proof, said the prosecutors, had not been met in this case.

Impeachable Offenses?

The president's attorneys finished by arguing that whatever wrong Clinton had done was far short of the great calamity the founding fathers had envisioned when they put the impeachment clause in the Constitution.

"If you convict and remove President Clinton on the basis of these allegations," warned Craig, "no President of the United States will ever be safe from impeachment again."[71]

The president's attorneys pointed out that impeachment of the president could not be compared with cases in which judges were impeached. A judge, after all, was not elected but appointed for life. Impeachment was the only way of getting a bad judge out of office. A president, on the other hand, faced election every four years. If the American people did not like his performance, they could vote him out of office. "Removal must be an act of last resort when the political process can no longer protect the nation." [72]

Ruff took dead aim at Hyde's appeal to patriotism—his reference to the beaches of Normandy. "My father was on Omaha Beach 55 years ago," he said to a hushed Senate. "He didn't fight, no one fought, for one side of this case or the other. He fought as all those did for our country and our Constitution." [73]

Plea from a Senator

Clinton's team chose ex-senator Dale Bumpers to complete their defense with an appeal to his former colleagues. Bumpers asked the senators to keep a sense of proportion about the case. Perjurers were in prison because they lied about serious matters such as murder. This was a case of trying to cover up a private affair to protect a family from embarrassment. The issue came up only because of a relentless, out-of-control investigation, "maybe the most intense investigation not only of a president but of anybody, ever." [74]

Dale Bumpers, chosen by Clinton's team to complete their defense, urged senators to realize that Clinton had suffered for his actions and to end the trial.

No one should feel that Clinton had gotten away with his actions, according to Bumpers. The affair had devastated his family and had caused him more shame than most people would experience in a lifetime. Bumpers finished by reminding the senators that they were elected to serve the voters. "The American people, now and for some time, have been asking for a good night's sleep," said Bumpers. "They're asking for an end to this nightmare. It is a legitimate request." [75]

Back to the Witnesses

The president's team had succeeded in raising serious doubts about the House managers' case. People on both sides became convinced that, based on all the evidence that had been presented, the Senate would not convict Clinton. That made the unresolved matter of whether to call witnesses more important than ever. The House managers believed witnesses were crucial to their case. They believed that the only way they could expose the lies and obstruction of justice was to put the main characters in this cover-up under oath before the Senate. Then the senators could hear for themselves the contradictions, the half-truths, and the verbal smokescreens. Perhaps one of the witnesses protecting the president would crack and establish the president's guilt once and for all.

The House managers asked the Senate to simply abide by the established rules. In all previous impeachment cases, the Senate had allowed the House managers to present any evidence and witnesses they felt were needed to establish their case. In the Andrew Johnson impeachment trial, the House managers had called nineteen witnesses.

The Senate had an obligation to listen to all the evidence against the accused, said the House managers. No court in the nation would try to judge a case without hearing from the witnesses involved.

The Democrats repeated their argument that the testimony was already available, in excruciating detail. The only point in bringing in witnesses would be to prolong the embarrassing affair. The American people had made it clear that they wanted this brought to a close. They did not want the Senate to disgrace itself by probing every sordid detail of the case. Senator John Kerrey of Massachusetts argued strongly against calling witnesses, explaining, "We think that would really become a zoo and seriously prolong the process, unnecessarily so." [76]

Open Debate

Meanwhile, another argument was taking place. Democratic senators Harkin and Paul Wellstone of Minnesota wanted the Senate's debate over the evidence prior to the final vote to be open to the public. They noted that the tradition of closed-door debate established in the Johnson impeachment was no longer valid because it had taken place in an era when the Senate did much of its work in secret. Harkin and Wellstone argued that the American public had a right to hear what its elected officials had to say about the matter.

Republican senator Mitch McConnell of Kentucky led the opposition to open debate. He argued that senators would be more honest and open in a closed debate than they would if they were performing for television cameras. In the end, McConnell's side won, and the Senate decreed that the final debate would be behind closed doors.

Byrd's Bombshell

While the debates over witnesses and procedures were under way, the partisan bickering that Republicans and Democrats had hoped to avoid began surfacing. When senators were invited to submit written questions to both the House managers and the president's defense team, their questions almost invariably took the form of defending the president or attacking him.

Any pretense that the impeachment process would be a bipartisan exercise vanished with a proposal by Democrat Robert Byrd of West Virginia. Both parties had been courting favor with Byrd. One of the longest-serving senators in office, he was widely regarded as the expert on the traditions of the Senate. If Byrd voted to impeach Clinton, his influence could conceivably tilt the balance in favor of impeachment. Prior to this, Byrd had given no indication of which way he was leaning on the issue.

THE MAVERICKS

In the end, the Senate vote on the impeachment resolutions was nearly as politically divided as the House vote had been. But there were a few senators who crossed party lines in their votes.

The only Democrat to do so was Russ Feingold of Wisconsin. Feingold had made a name for himself with bold stands, most notably his refusal to accept any money from political action groups. That refusal nearly cost him reelection in 1998. While Feingold voted to acquit Clinton in the end, he gained notoriety by voting against Byrd's move to dismiss the trial.

Some dismissed the vote as just another example of Feingold's efforts to attract attention by being different. Feingold responded by saying, "This whole notion of being a maverick is not an accurate account of what I was doing here. I am simply trying to vote what I think is right."

Five Republicans responded similarly after they voted to acquit Clinton of both charges. One of the five, Arlen Specter of Pennsylvania, took the case very seriously, going to the extreme of launching his own investigation to determine whether White House aide Michael Blumenthal lied in his testimony to the Senate. A former prosecutor, Specter held a very strict legal standard of guilt. According to that standard, the House managers had not proved the president guilty of the charges. Specter had his doubts about Clinton and tried to vote "not proven" instead of "not guilty," but his vote was counted as being in favor of acquittal. The other four Republicans who voted to acquit on both charges were from the Northeast: Olympia Snowe and Susan Collins from Maine, John Chaffee of Rhode Island, and James Jeffords of Vermont. Five other Republicans, from a wider cross-section of the nation, voted to convict on the obstruction-of-justice charge but to acquit on the perjury charge. They were Richard Shelby of Alabama, Ted Stevens of Alaska, Fred Thompson of Tennessee, John Warner of Virginia, and Slade Gorton of Washington.

But on January 22, Byrd announced that he felt "lengthening the trial will only prolong and deepen the divisive, bitter, and polarizing effect that this sorry affair has visited upon our nation." [77]

Byrd's announcement stunned Republicans. Although they defeated the motion to dismiss, all but one Democrat voted in favor of it. Republicans could see that, with the Democrats now united in opposing impeachment, there was no longer any realistic

In order to avoid prolonging a trial that he believed was detrimental to society, influential senator Robert Byrd announced that he felt it was time to dismiss the matter.

chance of ousting Clinton from office. Even Pat Robertson, an influential conservative leader, publicly stated that the case was lost. He advised Republicans to dismiss it quickly and get on with other legislative matters.

Finding of Fact

Republican senators were inclined to take Robertson's advice. But they faced a ticklish problem: How could they drop the case without making the House managers look bad? The managers had argued strongly that allowing Clinton to remain in office posed a danger to the nation and to the Constitution. If the Senate simply voted without any further testimony, it would seem as though they were admitting that the House Republicans had exaggerated and had let personal hatred of Clinton blind them to the realities of the case.

Moderate Republican senators Susan Collins and Olympia Snowe of Maine, suggested the idea of a "finding of fact." This would allow the senators to declare Clinton guilty of some of the charges brought by the House and would condemn his behavior. However, it would not formally convict the president of

IMPEACHMENT EFFECT ON KOSOVO

How much did the Clinton impeachment hurt the country? There is no way to measure the impact, but the question has led to some interesting speculation. The war in Kosovo is one example.

In the spring of 1999, police and armed forces of the Yugoslavian government entered the province of Kosovo. These forces, made up of ethnic Serbians, began a campaign of brutality against the ethnic Albanian majority that lived in Kosovo. Leaders of the North Atlantic Treaty Organization (NATO), which included the United States, warned Yugoslavian president Slobodan Milosevic to stop the violence and seek a peaceful solution to tensions in Kosovo. When he did not, NATO began a campaign of air strikes against Yugoslavia.

Milosevic responded by stepping up the campaign of terror, killing untold numbers of Kosovars and driving more than half a million of them from their homes. As the NATO bombing continued, critics charged that the U.S. policy was poorly thought out and the operations poorly planned. Some began to question whether Clinton had been too distracted by his impeachment problems at the beginning of the year to properly prepare for the confrontation with Yugoslavia. For example, no U.S. ground forces were anywhere near Yugoslavia when the bombing began, denying NATO the threat of an invasion.

Similarly, an investigation late in the spring of 1999 revealed that Chinese spies had been stealing U.S. nuclear weapons secrets for years and that the federal government had ignored at least some indications that this was happening. Again, critics wondered, would the government have been more alert had officials not been preoccupied with the furor over impeachment?

The lack of trust that resulted from the president's deceit in the Lewinsky scandal made his job even more difficult than usual. Clinton had trouble mustering support from many people who normally would have rallied around the president in times of military crisis. Republicans in Congress refused to endorse the president's actions in Kosovo. Even those who agreed that Milosevic was a tyrant who needed to be stopped questioned Clinton's policies. As one of them said, "A discredited president has a hard time leading, even when it's for the right reasons."

the impeachment charges and so would make no attempt to re-move him from office. Snowe and Collins hoped that this option would hold the president accountable for his actions without taking the step that most Americans thought was too drastic a punishment for what Clinton had done.

This option, however, ran into fierce opposition from both Republicans and Democrats. They pointed out that the Senate could not simply make up its own rules when it did not like the options established in the Constitution. The House had brought forth impeachment charges; the Senate's job was to decide whether the president was guilty or not. If it found him guilty, the Constitution required that he be removed from office.

Last Chance for the House Managers

On January 27, the Senate Republicans made the smallest con-cession to their colleagues in the House in the hope of providing some face-saving cover for them. The Senate voted to allow only three witnesses. Monica Lewinsky would testify about her rela-tionship to Clinton and what the president might have said to in-fluence her to submit a false affidavit. Vernon Jordan would testify about the timing of and the reasoning behind his efforts to find a job for Lewinsky. White House aide Michael Blumen-thal would answer questions about false statements Clinton had given him about his relationship with Lewinsky.

To avoid the possibility of embarrassing sexual details being drawn and besmirching the dignity of the Senate, the witnesses would give their testimony, or depositions, on videotape. The House managers were livid at the restriction. They had always believed that their best chance of gaining a conviction was for the senators to hear the live testimony of witnesses and then de-termine from that who was telling the truth. Now they were re-duced to a paper-thin hope that somehow one of the witnesses, all of whom were Clinton supporters, would crack and come out with statements that cast doubt on the president.

That did not happen. *Newsweek* described the questioning of Monica Lewinsky by Representative Ed Bryant of Tennessee as "hapless." "Seems to me that *she* was deposing *him*,"[78] commented

Democratic senator Ernest Hollings after viewing the videotape. Few of his colleagues actually took the time to view all the testimony.

Although the Senate then closed its doors and went into secret discussion of the case, there was no longer any suspense. It was obvious that the House managers would not come close to winning the two-thirds vote necessary to convict Clinton. The only question was whether the impeachment articles would win even a simple majority.

The Vote

On February 12, the Senate called roll. As each senator's name was read, he or she said either "guilty" or "not guilty." The perjury charge was defeated by a vote of fifty-five not guilty against forty-five guilty. The Senate deadlocked at an even split on obstruction of justice. Despite the exhausting efforts of both sides to avoid the party-line split that had torn apart the House, the vote went largely according to party loyalty. All forty-five Democrats voted against both impeachment articles. Only a few Republicans joined them.

After five weeks, the Senate impeachment trial was over. The American people could finally put to rest the scandal that had plagued the nation for over a year.

Paying the Price

Although his opponents complained that Clinton had gotten away with breaking the law, the president paid a price for his misdeeds. When asked if he was glad the scandal was finally over, Clinton said that it would never be over. His standing in history had been tarnished forever by the Lewinsky affair and his efforts to keep it secret. He had lost any chance of working with House Republicans on important national legislation. Because he had violated the trust of the American people, his motives and intentions would be called into question on virtually every issue that came before him.

Judge Wright delivered the most severe blow in the spring following the impeachment trial. She found Clinton in contempt of court for his testimony in the Paula Jones case and ordered him to pay fees to the court and to Jones's lawyers. "It simply is not acceptable to employ deceptions and falsehoods in an attempt to obstruct the judicial process," wrote Judge Wright. "There simply is no escaping the fact that the president deliberately violated this court's discovery orders and thereby undermined the integrity of the judicial system." [79]

Clinton's opponents also suffered badly. The House managers and Ken Starr had to endure scathing criticism that they had let their hatred of Clinton get in the way of common sense and decency. Ironically, the attempt to remove Clinton from office ended with Clinton still in office and two top Republican leaders, Newt Gingrich and Bob Livingston, forced to resign.

Some Republicans continued to hold out hope that history would come around to their point of view. "I think that eventually Republicans will be rewarded for doing the right thing," said one Republican strategist. "Now is that in two years or four or ten years? We don't know." [80] At least for the present, however, their role in pursuing the impeachment charges cost Republicans a great deal of respect among American voters.

In fact, the long scandal and bitter impeachment battle dealt the entire U.S. political system a damaging blow. Polls showed that about half of all Americans had a less favorable impression of their nation's political process because of the impeachment.

Lessons Learned from the Impeachment

The House managers had warned that the nation would be in deep trouble if Clinton remained in office. "If the President is not convicted as a consequence of the conduct that has been portrayed," they said, "then no House of Representatives will ever be able to impeach again and no Senate will ever convict. The bar will be so high that only a convicted felon or a traitor will need to be concerned." [81]

Some feared that Clinton's escape meant that the United States had lost its sense of right and wrong. Conservative activist Paul Weyrich declared, "I no longer believe there is a moral majority. I do not believe that a majority of Americans actually share our values." [82]

While some people worried that failure to impeach Clinton would send the wrong moral message, most believed that his misdeed was not serious enough to warrant removal from office.

But to the majority of Americans, the lesson of the impeachment attempt was that the nation's founders had been wise in setting up the impeachment process. Impeachment has to be reserved for those cases in which a president has so abused his power that he poses a danger to the nation. The American people did not approve of Clinton's actions, but they also did not think those actions disqualified him from being president. They agreed with Republican Senator James Jeffords of Vermont, who said, "If you say lying about a noncrime can be converted into a high crime by the way you handle it, that sets a pretty low standard." [83]

Whether the Republicans were right or wrong in saying that Clinton had committed impeachable offenses, the American people were as suspicious of their motives as they were of Clinton's testimony. The trial of Bill Clinton showed that the Constitution makes it very difficult for any party to use impeachment to get rid of a president they do not feel is fit to continue in office. Impeachment can succeed only if people in both parties throughout the country lose faith in their president and demand his removal.

Notes

Introduction: An Agonizing Decision

1. Quoted in Michael Gerson and Kenneth T. Walsh, "Judgment Day," *U.S. News & World Report*, December 21, 1998, p. 22.
2. Quoted in Francis X. Clines, "A Dreadful Day Unfolds," *New York Times*, December 19, 1998, p. A-1.
3. Quoted in Jodi Wilgren, "For Fence-Sitter, Pressure from Within," *New York Times*, December 16, 1998, p. A-32.

Chapter 1: History of Impeachment

4. Quoted in John Lobovitz, *Presidential Impeachment.* New Haven, CT: Yale University Press, 1978, p. 3.
5. Quoted in Lobovitz, *Presidential Impeachment*, p. 4.
6. Quoted in Lobovitz, *Presidential Impeachment*, p. 4.
7. Quoted in Lobovitz, *Presidential Impeachment*, p. 8.
8. Quoted in Jonathan Alter, "Censure and Move On," *Newsweek*, December 21, 1998, p. 28.
9. Quoted in Lobovitz, *Presidential Impeachment*, p. 8.
10. Quoted in William Kristol, "Impeach and Convict," *Newsweek*, December 21, 1998, p. 28.
11. Quoted in Gene Smith, *High Crimes and Misdemeanors: The Impeachment and Trial of Andrew Johnson.* New York: Morrow, 1977, p. 190.
12. Quoted in Smith, *High Crimes and Misdemeanors*, p. 60.
13. Quoted in Smith, *High Crimes and Misdemeanors*, p. 218.
14. Quoted in Smith, *High Crimes and Misdemeanors*, pp. 191, 241.

Chapter 2: The Crime

15. Quoted in Jeffrey Rosen, "Kenneth Starr," *New York Times Magazine*, June 1, 1997, p. 45.
16. Quoted in Mark Steyn, "All Deliberative Speed," *National Review*, February 22, 1999, p. 25.
17. Quoted in Eric Alterman, "The C Word (and It's Not Clinton)," *National Review*, December 7, 1998, p. 5.

Chapter 3: Punishing the President

18. Quoted in Richard Lowry, "Starmageddan," *National Review*, December 12, 1998, p. 6.

19. Elise Ackerman, "Perjury and the President," *U.S. News & World Report*, October 5, 1998, p. 23.

20. Quoted in Brian Kelly and Major Garrett, "Will This Play Ever End?" *U.S. News & World Report*, November 30, 1998, p. 24.

21. Quoted in *Newsweek*, "Dash: Why I Left Starr," November 30, 1998, p. 26.

22. Quoted in Raja Mishra, "Panel Impeachment Vote Nears," *Leader-Telegram* (Eau Claire, Wisconsin), December 7, 1998, p. A-2.

23. Major Garrett, "Impeachment Blues," *U.S. News & World Report*, November 23, 1998, p. 28.

24. Quoted in Mishra, "Panel Impeachment Vote Nears,"p. A-1.

25. Quoted in Gerson and Walsh, "Judgment Day,"p. 23.

26. Quoted in Laurie Kellman, "Democrat Slams Foray into Clinton's Fund Raising," *Leader-Telegram* (Eau Claire, Wisconsin), December 1, 1998, p. A-1.

Chapter 4: The House Struggles with Impeachment

27. Quoted in *National Review*, "Throwback," January 25, 1998, p. 24.

28. Quoted in *New York Times*, "Excerpts from the Statement of Judicial Panel Majority Counsel," December 17, 1998, p. A-32.

29. Quoted in Lizette Alvarez, "A Solemn Hearing," *New York Times*, December 11, 1998, p. A-1.

30. Quoted in Kenneth T. Walsh, "A Fight to the Finish," *U.S. News & World Report*, October 19, 1998, p. 22.

31. Quoted in Alvarez, "A Solemn Hearing," p. A-1.

32. Quoted in Jill Abramson, "Mixed Reaction to Rebuttal That Is More Detailed," *New York Times*, December 9, 1998, p. A-23.

33. Quoted in Walsh, "A Fight to the Finish," p. 22.

34. Quoted in Kelly and Garrett, "Will This Play Ever End?" p. 24.

35. Quoted in Lizette Alvarez and John Broder, "Defenders of President Take Their Case to the House Judiciary Committee," *New York Times*, December 9, 1998, p. A-22.

36. Quoted in Alter, "Censure and Move On," p. 28.

37. David Gergen "It's Time for a Cease-Fire," *U.S. News & World Report*, January 4, 1999, p. 104.

38. Quoted in Ackerman, "Perjury and the President," p. 23.

39. Quoted in Neil A. Lewis, "Case Against President Would Fail," *New York Times*, December 10, 1998, p. A-25.

40. Quoted in Alvarez and Broder, "Defenders of President," p. A-22.

41. Quoted in Alvarez and Broder, "Defenders of President," p. A-22.

42. Quoted in Alvarez and Broder, "Defenders of President," p. A-22.

43. Quoted in Gerson and Walsh, "Judgment Day," p. 23.

44. Quoted in Ramesh Ponnuru, "Damage Estimate," *National Review*, February 8, 1999, p. 22.

45. Quoted in *New York Times*, "Impeachment Counts Unveiled," December 10, 1998, p. A-1.

46. Quoted in *New York Times*, "Impeachment Counts Unveiled," p. A-1.

47. Quoted in *New York Times*, "Impeachment Counts Unveiled," p. A-1.

48. Quoted in *U.S. News & World Report*, "We're All Hill Now," January 4, 1999, p. 30.

49. Quoted in *U.S. News & World Report*, "We're All Hill Now," p. 30.

50. Quoted in Francis X. Clines, "After the Vote, a Pause," *New York Times*, December 20, 1998, p. A-29.

51. Quoted in Gerson and Walsh, "Judgment Day," p. 23.

52 Gergen, "It's Time for a Cease-Fire," p. 104.

53. Quoted in John Broder and Lizette Alvarez, "White House Grasps at Options As Waverers Move to Impeach," *New York Times*, December 16, 1998, p. A-30.

54. Quoted in Alison Mitchell, "Will the Gentleman Yield a Minute to Bipartisanship? No!" *New York Times*, December 19, 1998, p. B-1.

55. Brian Duffy and Kenneth T. Walsh, "End Games," *U.S. News & World Report*, January 4, 1999, p. 20.

Chapter 5: The Senate Trial

56. Quoted in Gloria Berger, "Punishing One of Their Own," *U.S. News & World Report*, December 14, 1998, p. 31.

57. Quoted in Marianne Lavelle, "A Trial or a Deal?" *U.S. News & World Report*, January 4, 1999, p. 25.

58. Quoted in Lavelle, "A Trial or a Deal?" p. 26.

59. Quoted in Evan Thomas, "Why Clinton Won," *Newsweek*, February 22, 1999, p. 25.

60. Quoted in Lizette Alvarez and Eric Schmitt, "Opposition Emerges to Plan to Avert Full Trial of Clinton," *New York Times*, January 1, 1999, p. A-1.

61. Quoted in Neil A. Lewis, "Experts See No Parallel for Trial," *New York Times*, January 11, 1999, p. A-12.

62. Quoted in R. W. Apple Jr., "Senate Hears First Pleas by House to Remove Clinton," *New York Times*, January 15, 1999, pp. A-1, A-15.

63. Quoted in Alison Mitchell, "A Day's Forceful Subtext," *New York Times*, January 15, 1999, p. A-1.

64. Quoted in Neil A. Lewis, "Prosecutors Take Advantage of Broad Obstruction of Justice Statutes," *New York Times*, January 15, 1999, p. A-13.

65. Quoted in Apple, "Senate Hears First Pleas," p. A-14.

66. Quoted in *New York Times*, "The Charges: 'This Is About a Scheme, This Is About a Lot of Lies,'" January 16, 1999, p. A-12.

67. Quoted in R. W. Apple Jr., "Prosecution Argues Impeachment of Clinton's Deeds," *New York Times*, January 17, 1999, p. A-27.

68. Quoted in Lizette Alvarez, "Harkin Wins Endorsement of Wider Role than Jury," *New York Times*, January 16, 1999, p. A-11.

69. Quoted in Apple, "Prosecution Argues Impeachment," pp. A-1, A-27.

Chapter 6: The Senate Decides

70. Quoted in R. W. Apple Jr., "Emphatic 'Not Guilty' Opens the Case for the Defense," *New York Times*, January 20, 1999, p. A-25.

71. Quoted in R. W. Apple Jr., "Defense Challenges Impeachment 'Mumbo Jumbo,'" *New York Times*, January 21, 1999, p. A-1.

72. Quoted in Apple, "Emphatic 'Not Guilty,'" p. A-27.

73. Quoted in Apple, "Emphatic 'Not Guilty,'" p. A-1.

74. Quoted in R. W. Apple Jr., "Eloquent Appeal," *New York Times*, January 22, 1999, p. A-18.

75. Quoted in Apple, "Eloquent Appeal," p. A-1.

76. Quoted in Alison Mitchell and Eric Schmitt, "Lott Says a Trial of Impeachment Begins Tomorrow," *New York Times*, January 6, 1999, p. A-20.

77. Quoted in *New York Times*, "Byrd's Statement on His Move to End Trial," January 23, 1999, p. A-11.

78. Quoted in Thomas, "Why Clinton Won," p. 31.

79. Quoted in Naftali Bendavid, "'Contempt' Branded on Clinton," *Leader-Telegram* (Eau Claire, Wisconsin), April 12, 1999, p. A-1.

80. Quoted in Ponnuru, "Damage Estimate," p. 22.

81. Quoted in James Bennett, "President Offers Formal Arguments Against Removal," *New York Times*, January 12, 1999, p. A-1.

82. Quoted in Alterman, "The C Word," p. 5.

83. Quoted in Lizette Alvarez and Eric Schmitt, "Gulf Widens After House Makes Case," *New York Times*, January 17, 1999, p. A-28.

Timeline

1868

The U.S. Senate acquits President Andrew Johnson of impeachment charges by a single vote.

1973

The U.S. House of Representatives prepares impeachment charges against President Richard Nixon, who resigns rather than face impeachment.

May 8, 1991

Paula Jones meets then-governor Bill Clinton at a hotel in Little Rock, Arkansas.

May 6, 1994

Paula Jones files a sexual harassment suit against President Bill Clinton based on events at the 1991 encounter.

August 1994

Special Counsel Kenneth Starr begins his investigation of the Whitewater real estate development.

May 27, 1997

The U.S. Supreme Court rules that a sitting president can be sued for actions that occurred before taking office.

Fall 1997

Linda Tripp begins secretly taping phone conversations with Monica Lewinsky that detail Lewinsky's affair with the president.

January 7, 1998

In an affidavit filed in the Jones suit, Lewinski denies any relationship with the president.

January 17, 1998

Clinton denies under oath any sexual relationship with Lewinsky.

August 17, 1998

Following public exposure of his relationship with Lewinsky, Clinton testifies via videotape before a grand jury.

September 10, 1998
Starr submits to Congress his report of possible impeachable offenses committed by Clinton.

September 30, 1998
The U.S. House of Representatives authorizes an impeachment inquiry into allegations against Clinton.

November 13, 1998
Jones agrees to settle her suit for $850,000.

December 19, 1998
The House of Representatives votes to impeach Clinton on two of the four articles brought by the House Judiciary Committee.

January 7, 1999
The U.S. Senate opens the impeachment trial of President Clinton.

January 22, 1999
Senator Robert Byrd announces he will file a motion to dismiss the case.

January 27, 1999
The U.S. Senate votes to allow only three witnesses to be questioned on videotape, drastically limiting the scope of the trial.

February 12, 1999
The Senate votes to acquit Clinton on both charges.

For Further Reading

Jonathan Alter, "Censure and Move On," *Newsweek*, December 21, 1998. In this editorial, Alter lays out the reasons why Clinton did not deserve to be impeached.

William Kristol, "Impeach and Convict," *Newsweek*, December 21, 1998. In this companion column to Alter's, Kristol states the case in favor of Clinton's impeachment.

John Lobovitz, *Presidential Impeachment*. New Haven, CT: Yale University Press, 1978. This book covers the history of efforts to impeach American presidents and includes a great deal of discussion on the founding fathers' debates over the issue of impeachment.

Gene Smith, *High Crimes and Misdemeanors: The Impeachment and Trial of Andrew Johnson*. New York: Morrow, 1977. This is a very readable account of the background and issues at stake in the impeachment trial of Andrew Johnson; it also covers the trial and behind-the-scenes activity and introduces many of the characters involved in the Senate trial.

Evan Thomas, "Why Clinton Won," *Newsweek*, February 22, 1999. This article sums up the Senate trial and explains why Clinton was acquitted of the impeachment charges.

Works Consulted

Jill Abramson, "Mixed Reaction to Rebuttal That Is More Detailed," *New York Times*, December 9, 1998.

Elise Ackerman, "Perjury and the President," *U.S. News & World Report*, October 5, 1998.

Eric Alterman, "The C World (and It's Not Clinton)," *National Review*, December 7, 1998.

Lizette Alvarez, "A Solemn Hearing," *New York Times*, December 11, 1998.

————, "Harkin Wins Endorsement of Wider Role than Jury," *New York Times*, January 16, 1999.

Lizette Alvarez and John Broder, "Defenders of President Take Their Case to the House Judiciary Committee," *New York Times*, December 9, 1998.

Lizette Alvarez and Eric Schmitt, "Gulf Widens After House Makes Case," *New York Times*, January 17, 1999.

————, "Opposition Emerges to Plan to Avert Full Trial of Clinton," *New York Times*, January 1, 1999.

R. W. Apple Jr., "Defense Challenges Impeachment 'Mumbo Jumbo,'" *New York Times*, January 21, 1999.

————, "Eloquent Appeal," *New York Times*, January 22, 1999.

————, "Emphatic 'Not Guilty' Opens the Case for the Defense," *New York Times*, January 20, 1999.

————, "Prosecution Argues Impeachment of Clinton's Deeds," *New York Times*, January 17, 1999.

————, "Senate Hears First Pleas by House to Remove Clinton," *New York Times*, January 15, 1999.

Naftali Bendavid, "'Contempt' Branded on Clinton," *Leader-Telegram* (Eau Claire, Wisconsin), April 12, 1999.

James Bennett, "President Offers Formal Arguments Against Removal," *New York Times*, January 12, 1999.

Gloria Berger, "Punishing One of Their Own," *U.S. News &*

World Report, December 14, 1998.

John Broder and Lizette Alvarez, "White House Grasps at Options As Waverers Move to Impeach," *New York Times*, December 16, 1998.

Francis X. Clines, "A Dreadful Day Unfolds," *New York Times*, December 19, 1998.

————, "After the Vote, a Pause," *New York Times*, December 20, 1998.

Brian Duffy and Kenneth T. Walsh, "End Games," *U.S. News & World Report*, January 4, 1999.

Major Garrett, "Impeachment Blues," *U.S. News & World Report*, November 23, 1998.

David Gergen, "It's Time for a Cease-Fire," *U.S. News & World Report*, January 4, 1999.

Michael Gerson and Kenneth T. Walsh, "Judgment Day," *U.S. News & World Report*, December 21, 1998.

Laurie Kellman, "Democrat Slams Foray into Clinton's Fund Raising," *Leader-Telegram* (Eau Claire, Wisconsin), December 1, 1998.

Brian Kelly and Major Garrett, "Will This Play Ever End?" *U.S. News & World Report*, November 30, 1998.

Marianne Lavelle, "A Trial or a Deal?" *U.S. News & World Report*, January 4, 1999.

Neil A. Lewis, "Case Against President Would Fail," *New York Times*, December 10, 1998.

————, "Experts See No Parallel for Trial," *New York Times*, January 11, 1999.

————, "Prosecutors Take Advantage of Broad Obstruction of Justice Statues," *New York Times*, January 15, 1999.

Richard Lowry, "Starmageddan," *National Review*, December 12, 1998.

Raja Mishra, "Panel Impeachment Vote Nears," *Leader-Telegram* (Eau Claire, Wisconsin), December 7, 1998.

Alison Mitchell, "A Day's Forceful Subtext," *New York Times*,

January 15, 1999.

———, "Will the Gentleman Yield a Minute to Bipartisanship? No!" *New York Times*, December 19, 1998.

Alison Mitchell and Eric Schmitt, "Lott Says a Trial of Impeachment Begins Tomorrow," *New York Times*, January 6, 1999.

National Review, "Throwback," January 25, 1998.

Newsweek, "Dash: Why I Left Starr," November 30, 1998, p. 26.

New York Times, "Byrd's Statement on His Move to End Trial," January 23, 1999.

———, "Excerpts from the Statement of Judicial Panel Majority Counsel," December 17, 1998.

———, "Impeachment Begins Tomorrow," January 6, 1999.

———, "Impeachment Counts Unveiled," December 10, 1998.

———, "The Charges: 'This Is About a Scheme, This Is About a Lot of Lies,'" January 16, 1999.

Ramesh Ponnuru, "Damage Estimate," *National Review*, February 8, 1999.

Jeffrey Rosen, "Kenneth Starr," *New York Times Magazine*, June 1, 1997.

Mark Steyn, "All Deliberative Speed," *National Review*, February 22, 1999.

U.S. News & World Report, "We're All Hill Now," January 4, 1999.

Kenneth T. Walsh, "A Fight to the Finish," *U.S. News & World Report*, October 19, 1998.

Jodi Wilgren, "For Fence-Sitter, Pressure from Within," *New York Times*, December 16, 1998.

Index

Picture Credits

Cover photo: © Erik Freeland/Matrix
Associated Press, 7, 30 (top), 35, 38, 40, 42 (top), 44, 51, 52, 55, 69, 78, 93
Corbis, 11, 19, 20
Corbis/AFP 8, 24, 26, 28, 29, 30 (bottom), 32, 46, 47, 50, 53, 58, 59, 62, 72, 81, 84, 88
Corbis/Wally McNamee, 74
Corbis/David Rubinger, 68
Corbis-Bettmann, 22, 42 (bottom)
Library of Congress, 12
pixelpartners, 16
Louis A. Warren Lincoln Library and Museum, 14

About the Author

Nathan Aaseng is the author of more than 140 books for young readers on a wide variety of subjects. More than three dozen of his works have won awards. A former microbiologist with a degree in biology and English from Luther College (Iowa), he currently lives in Eau Claire, Wisconsin, with his wife and four children.

OHIO COUNTY PUBLIC LIBRARY
WHEELING, W. VA. 26003